How to Draw
CHRiSTMaS
For kids
AF433549

WuTigerr is a brand name of Wutigerr LLC, represents multiple series of creative coloring books.

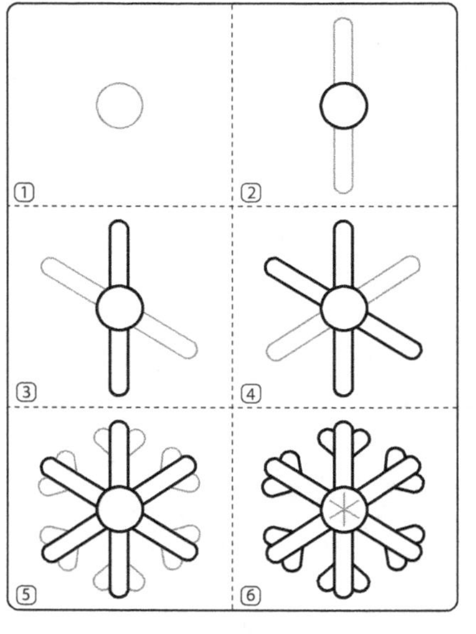
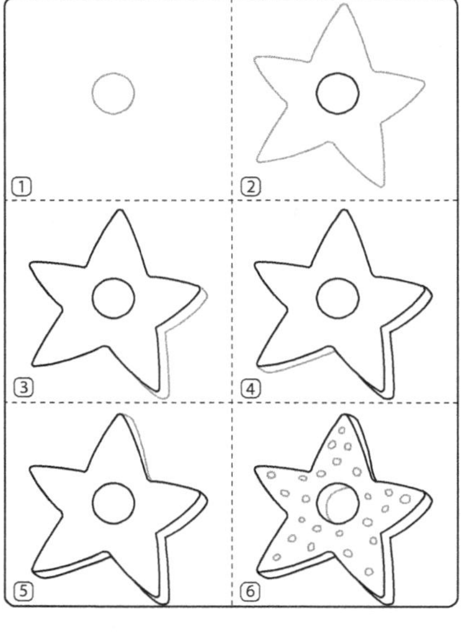
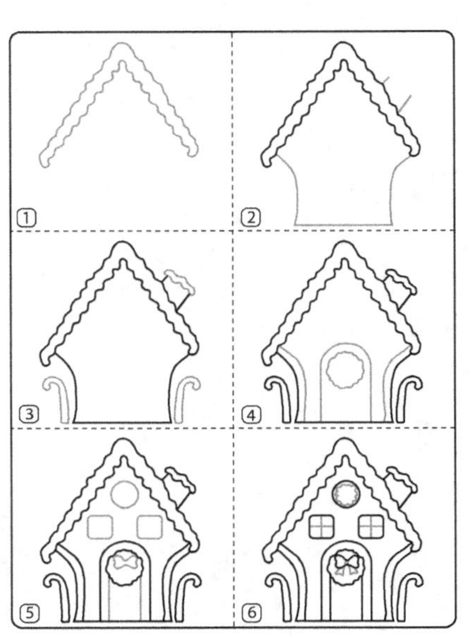

WU
TIGER
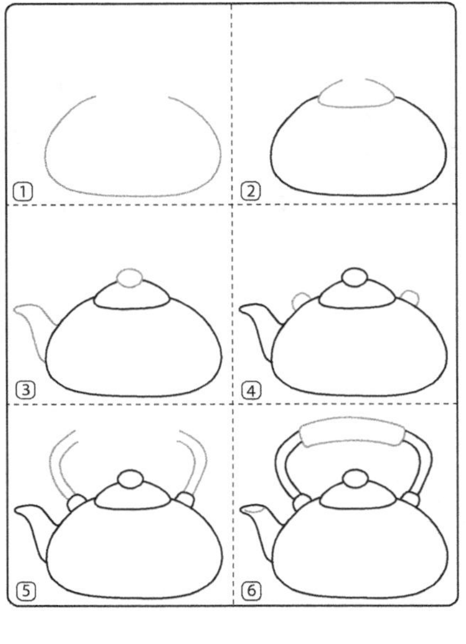
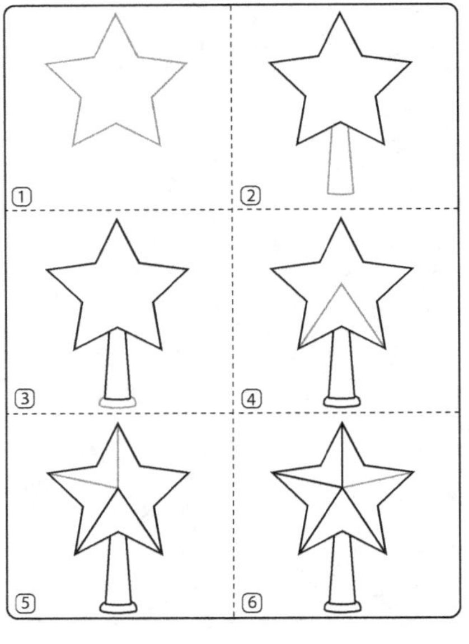

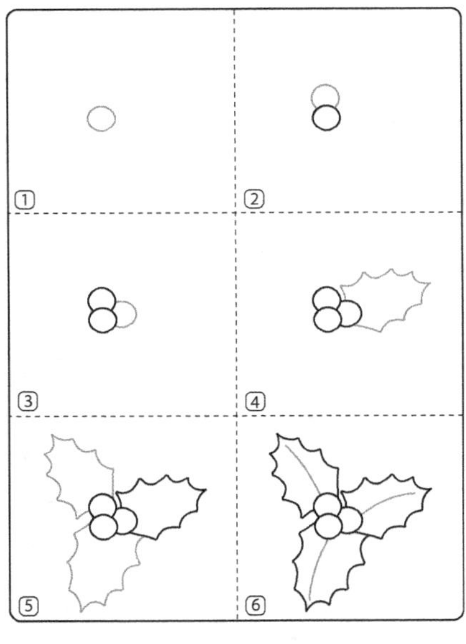

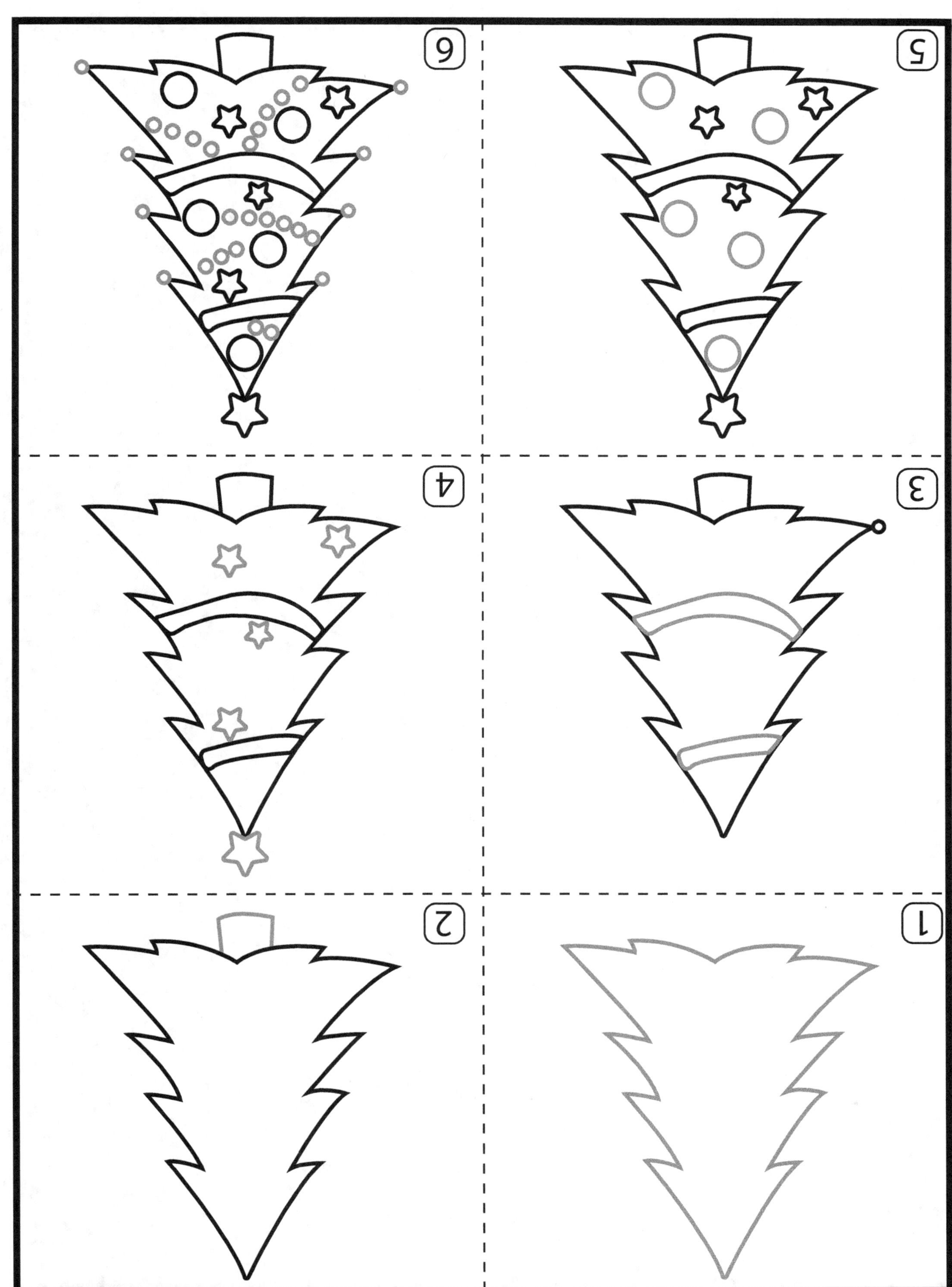

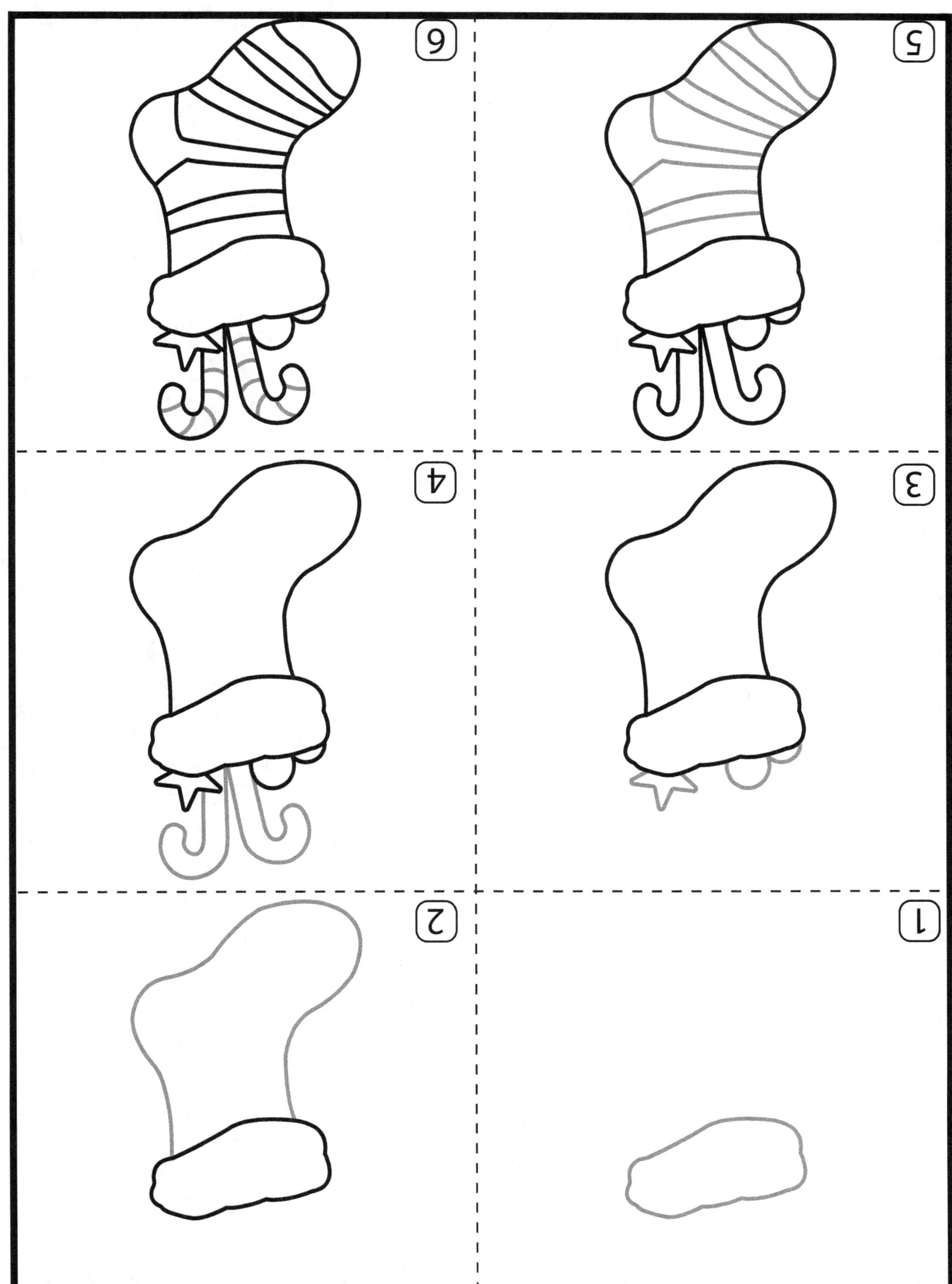

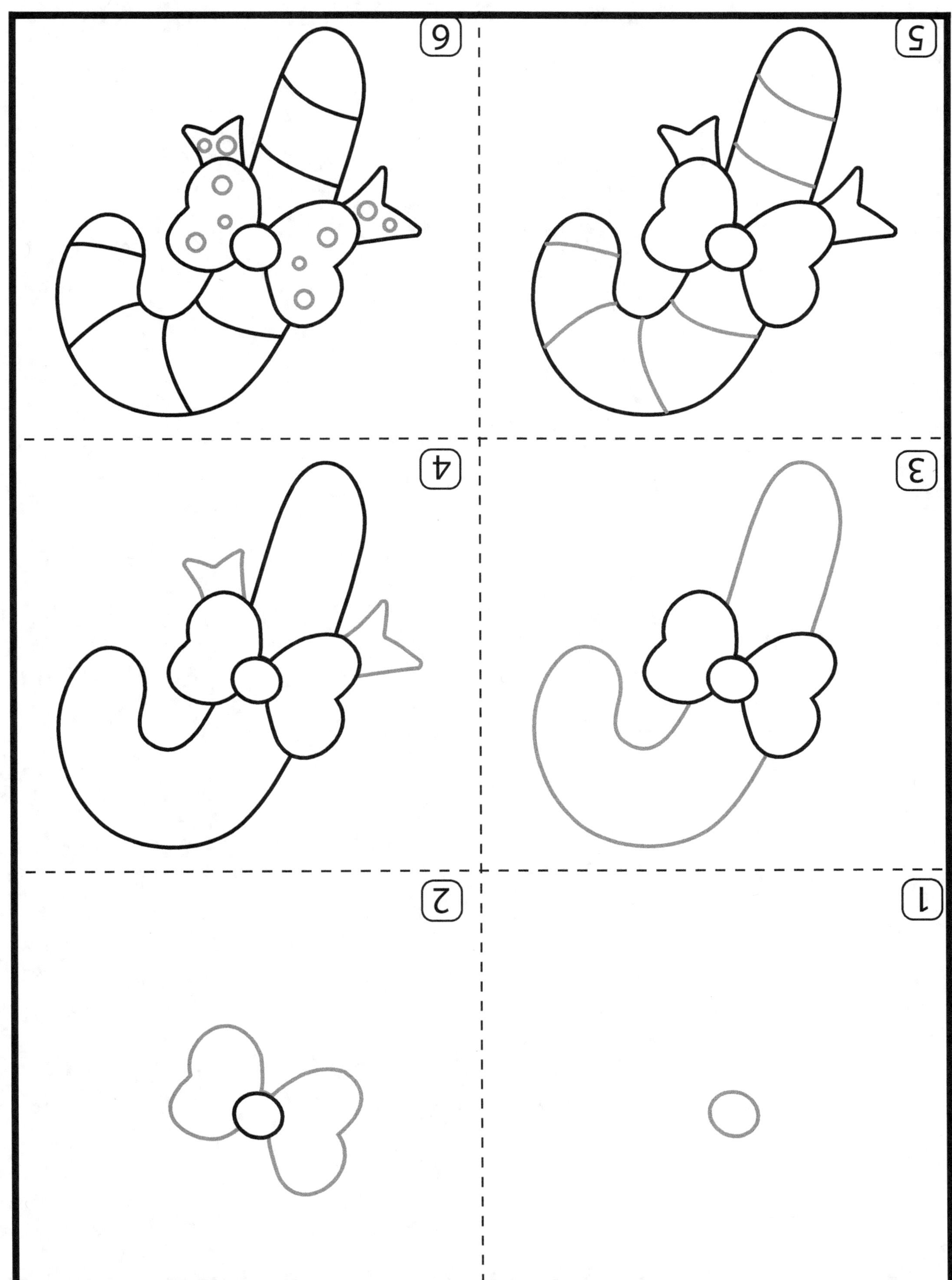

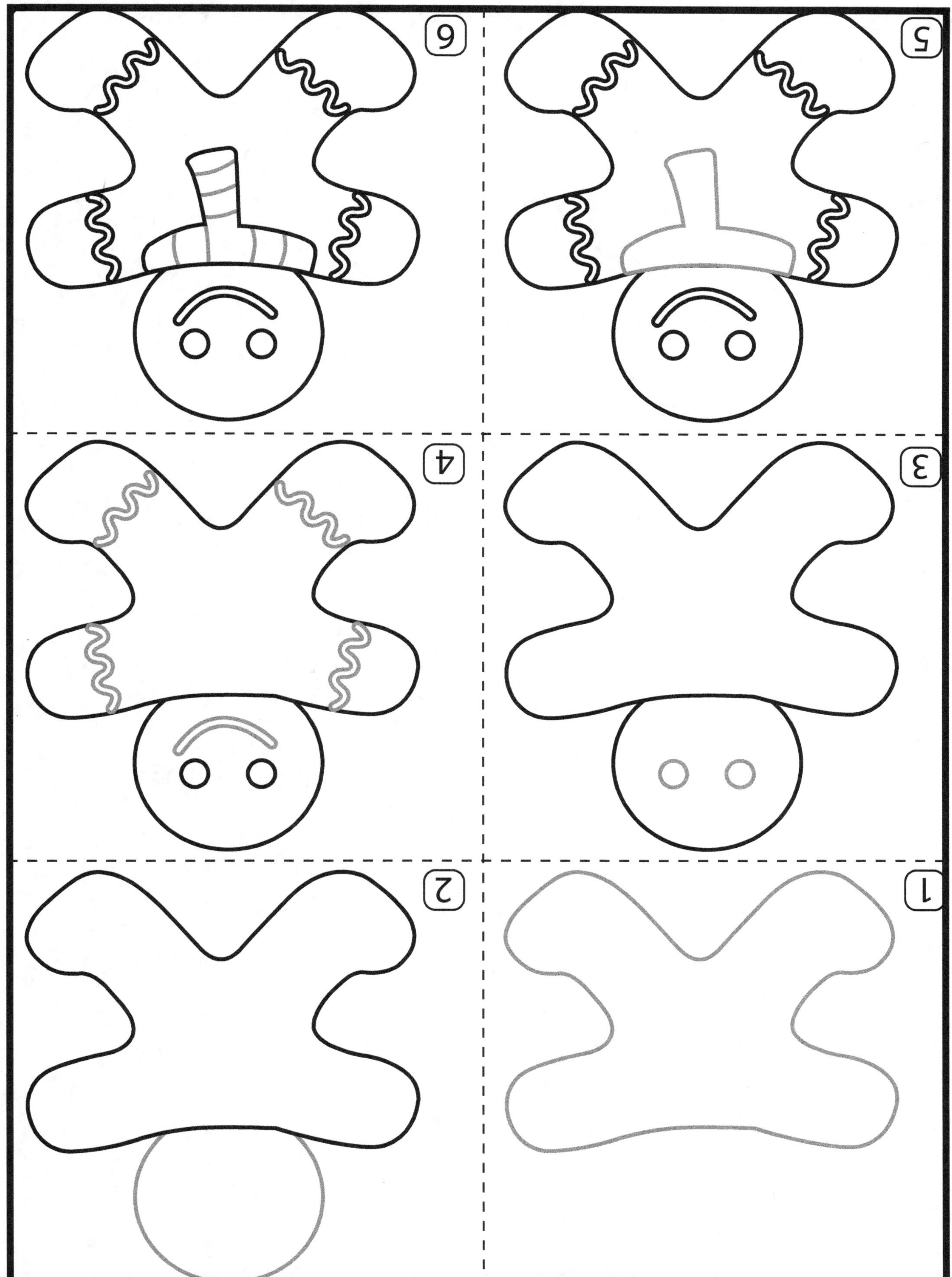

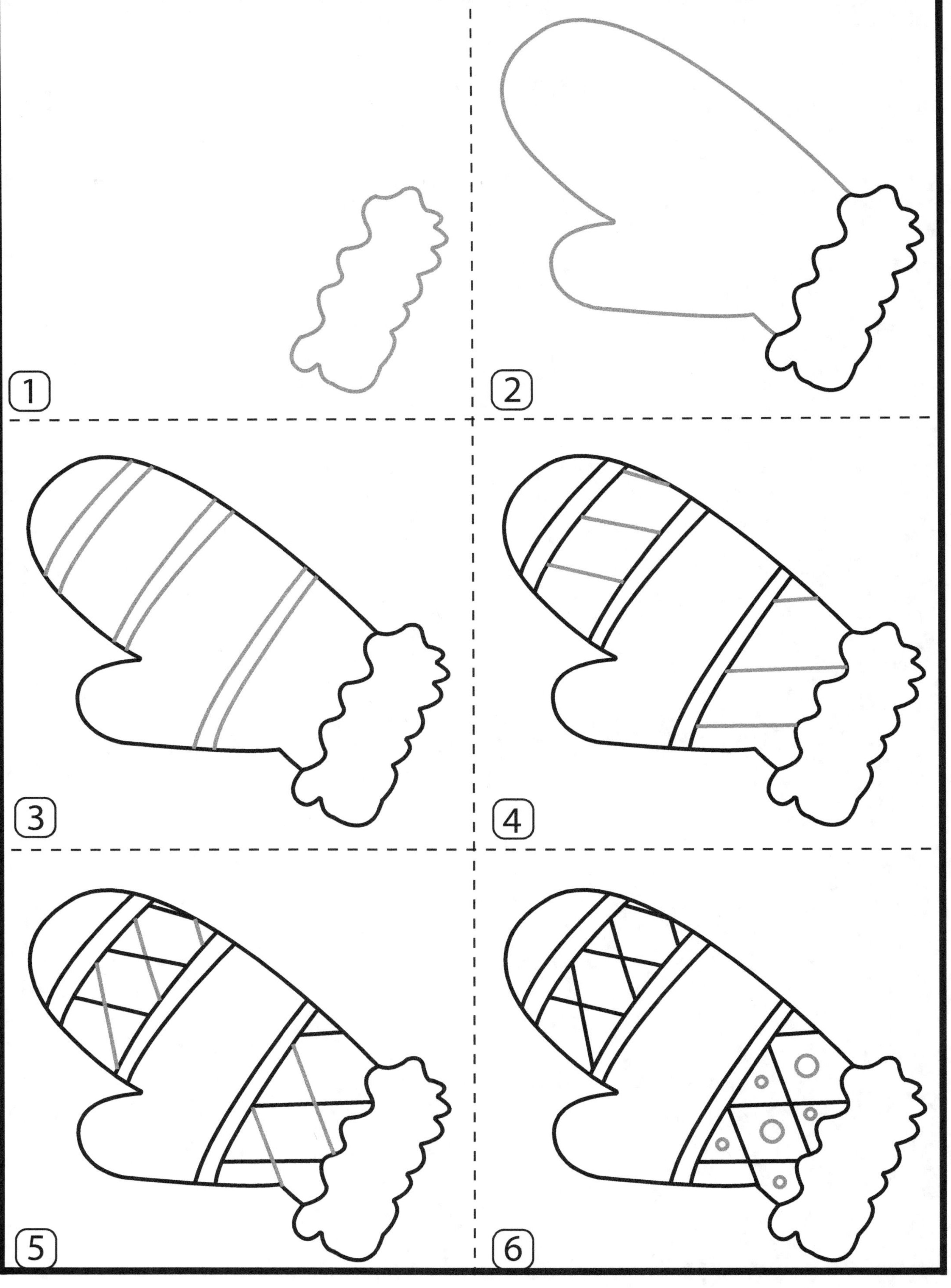

1
2
3
4
5
6

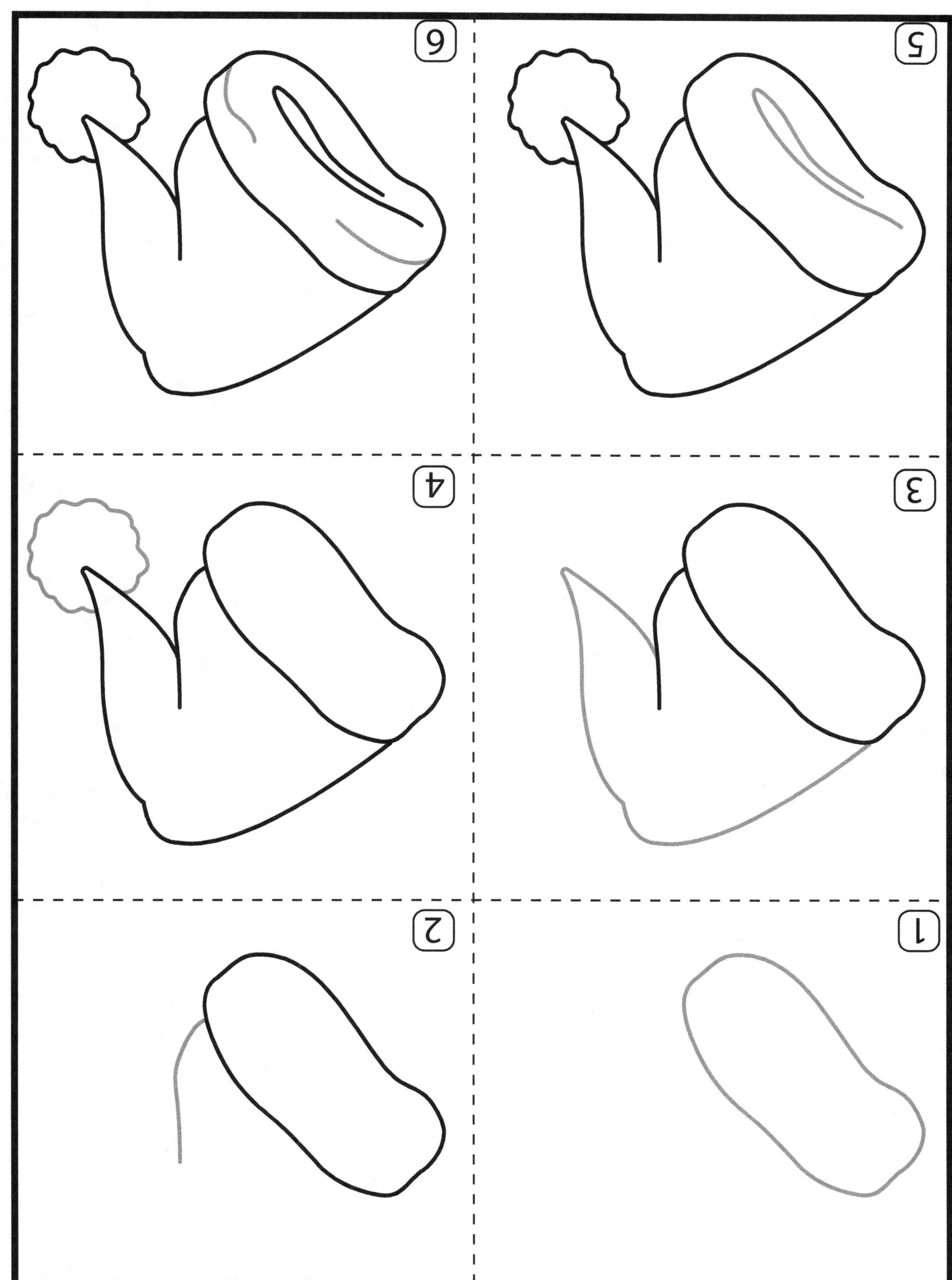

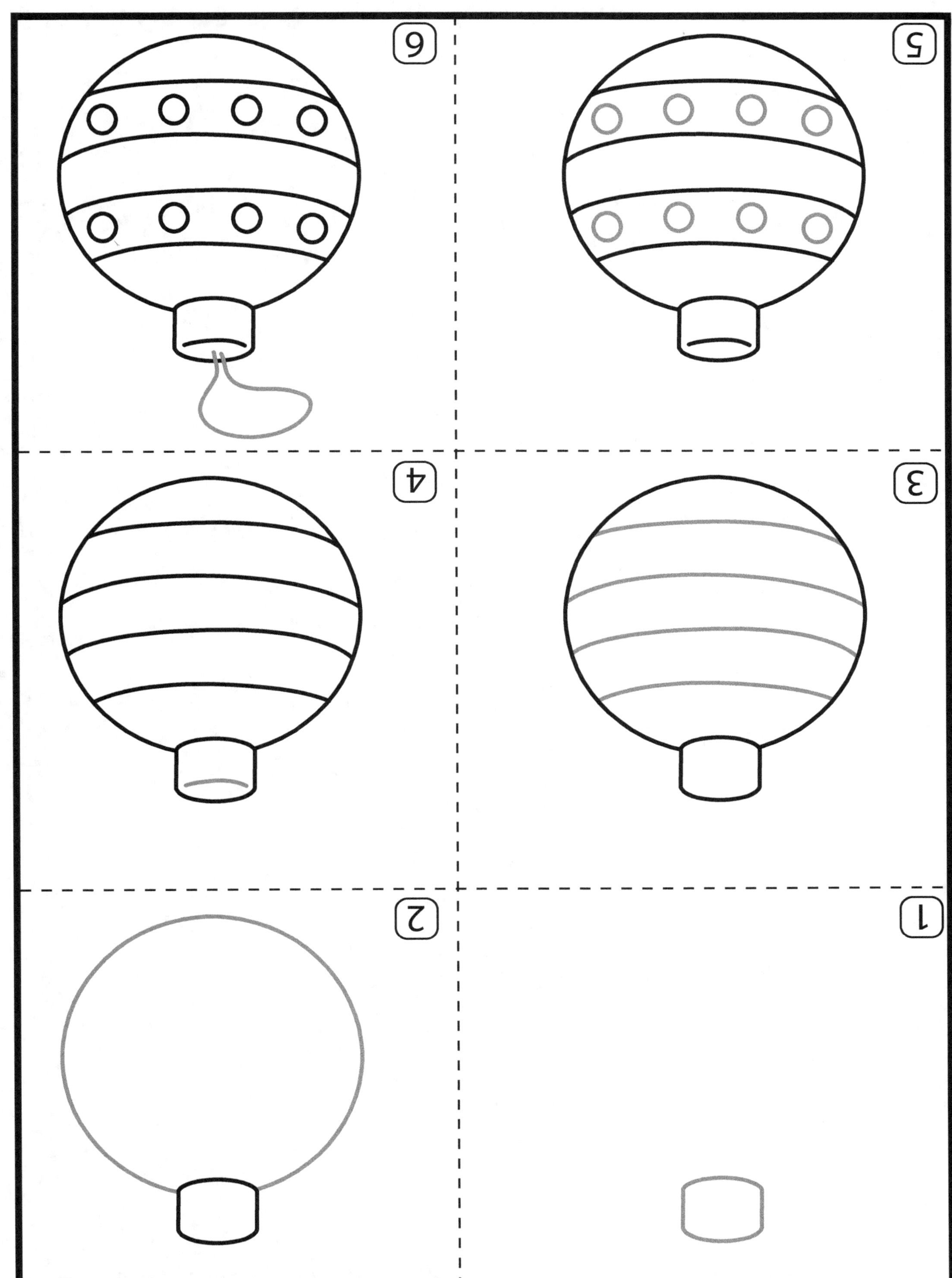

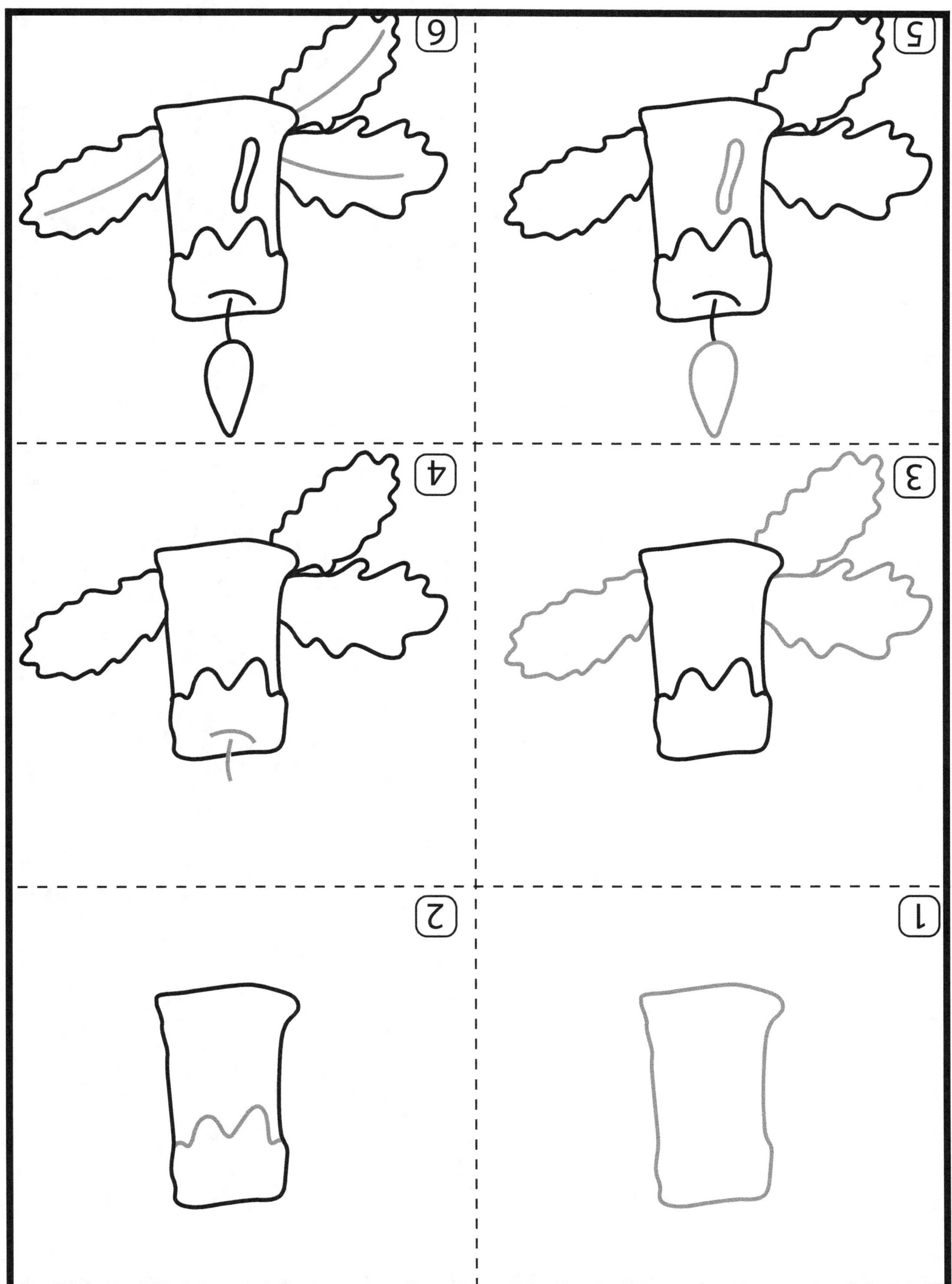

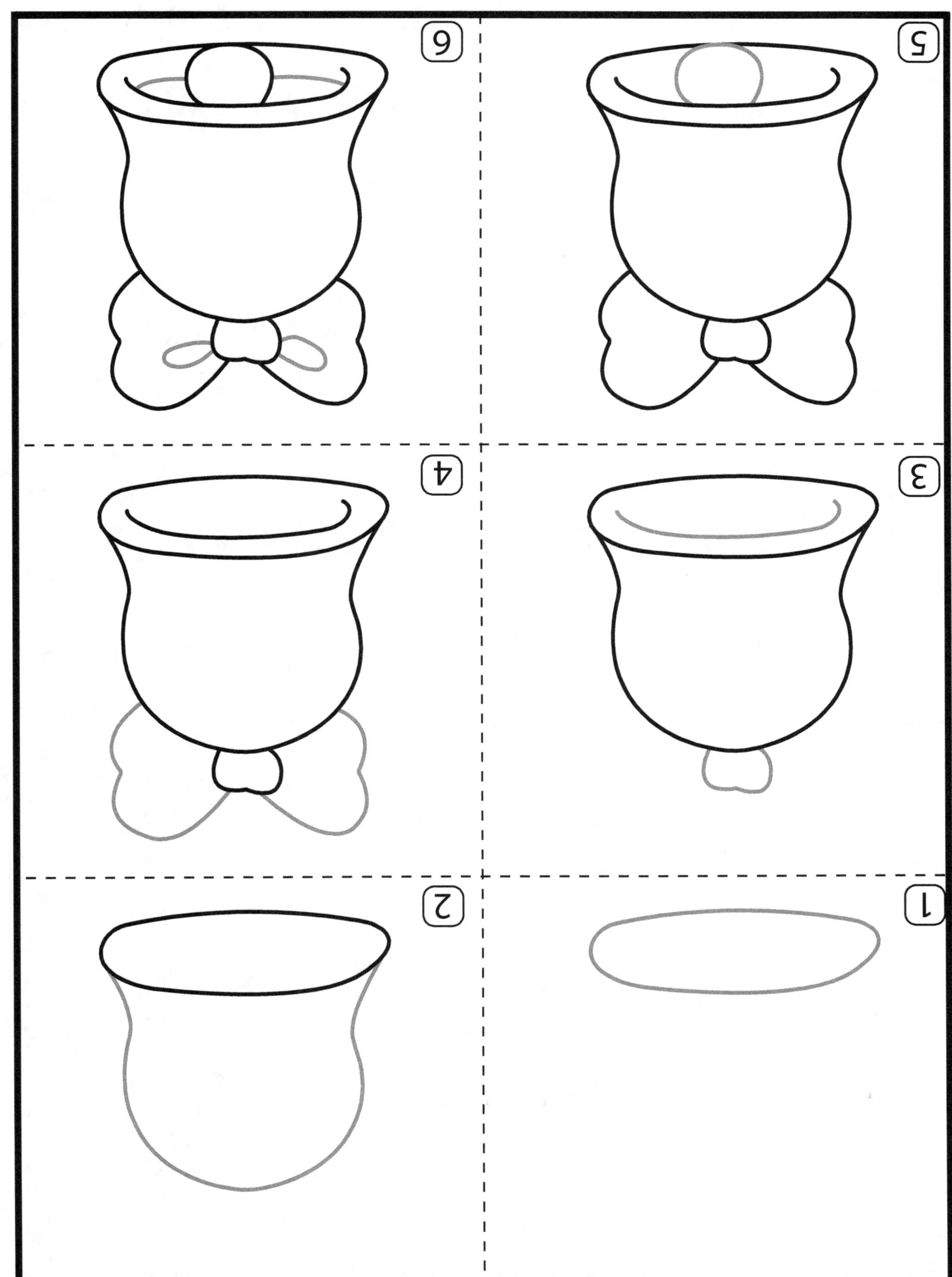

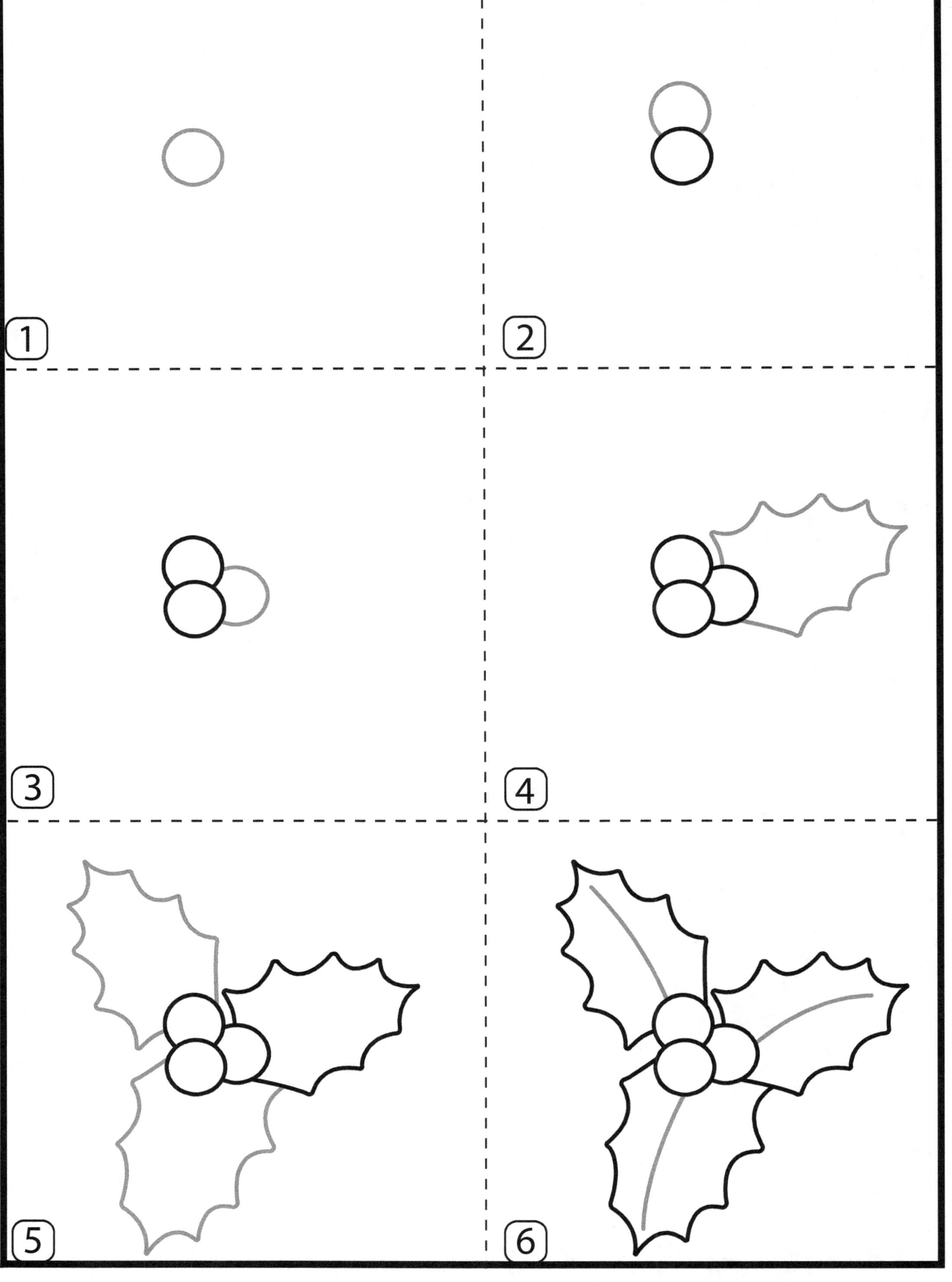

1
2
3
4
5
6

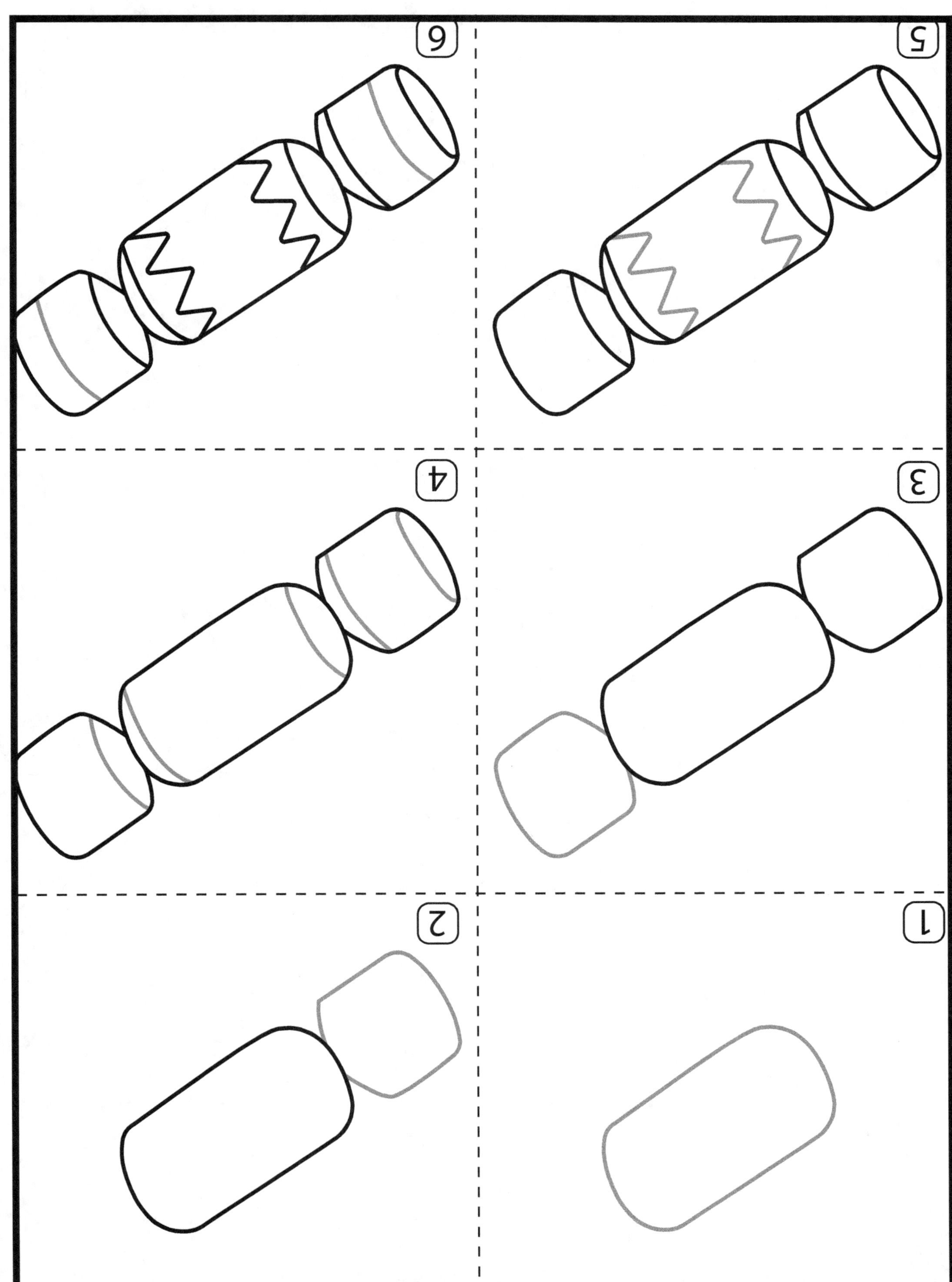

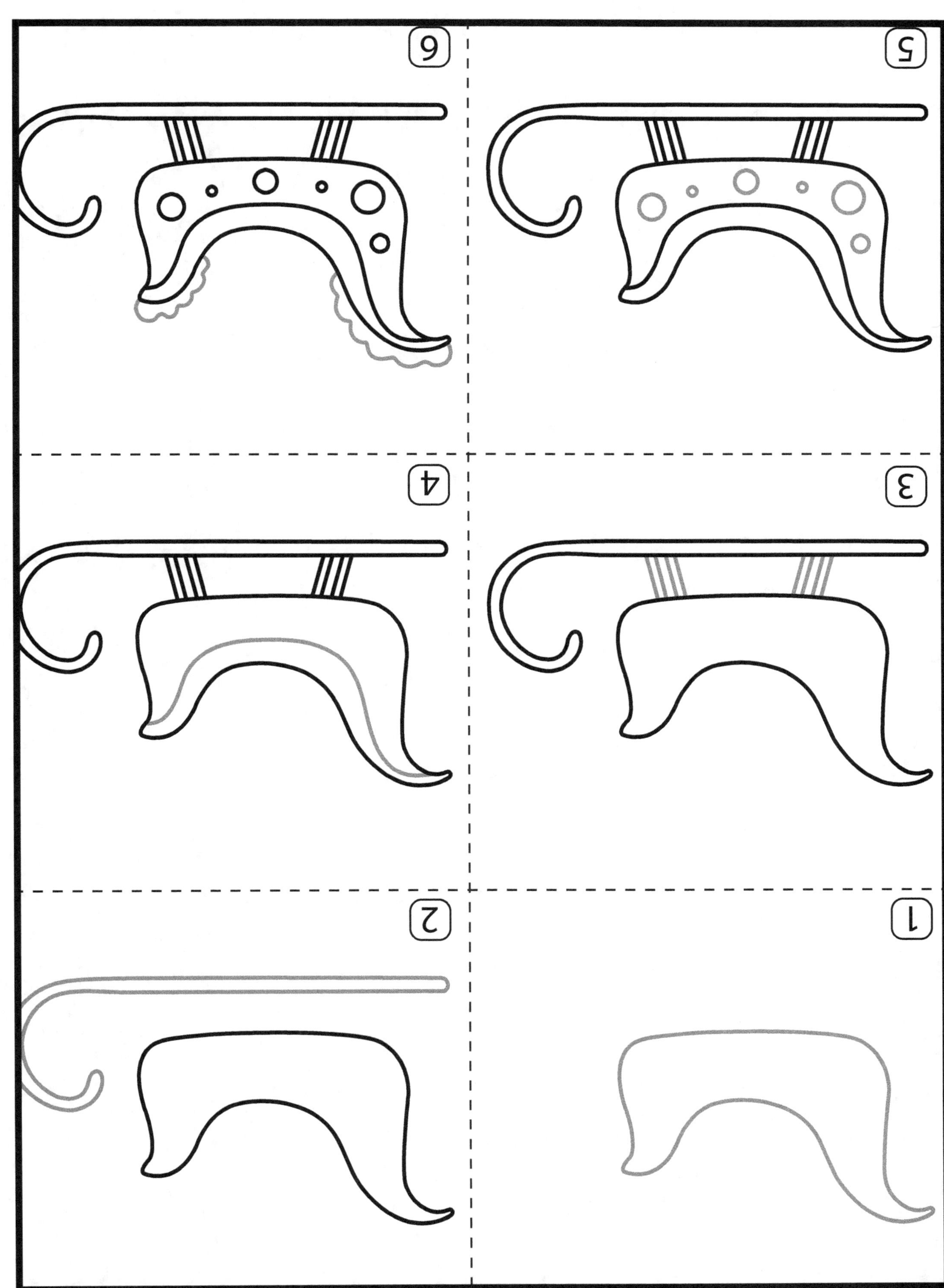

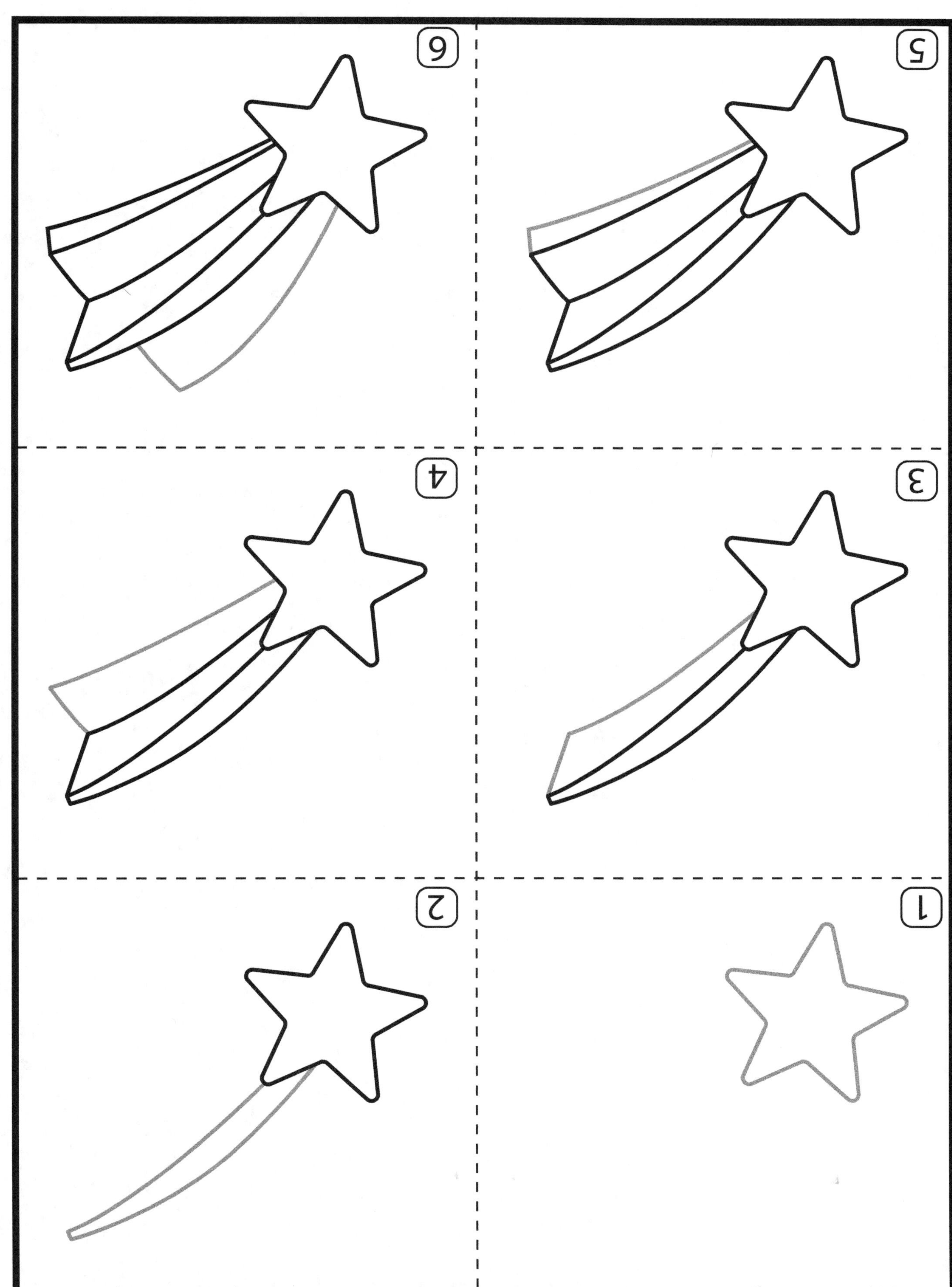

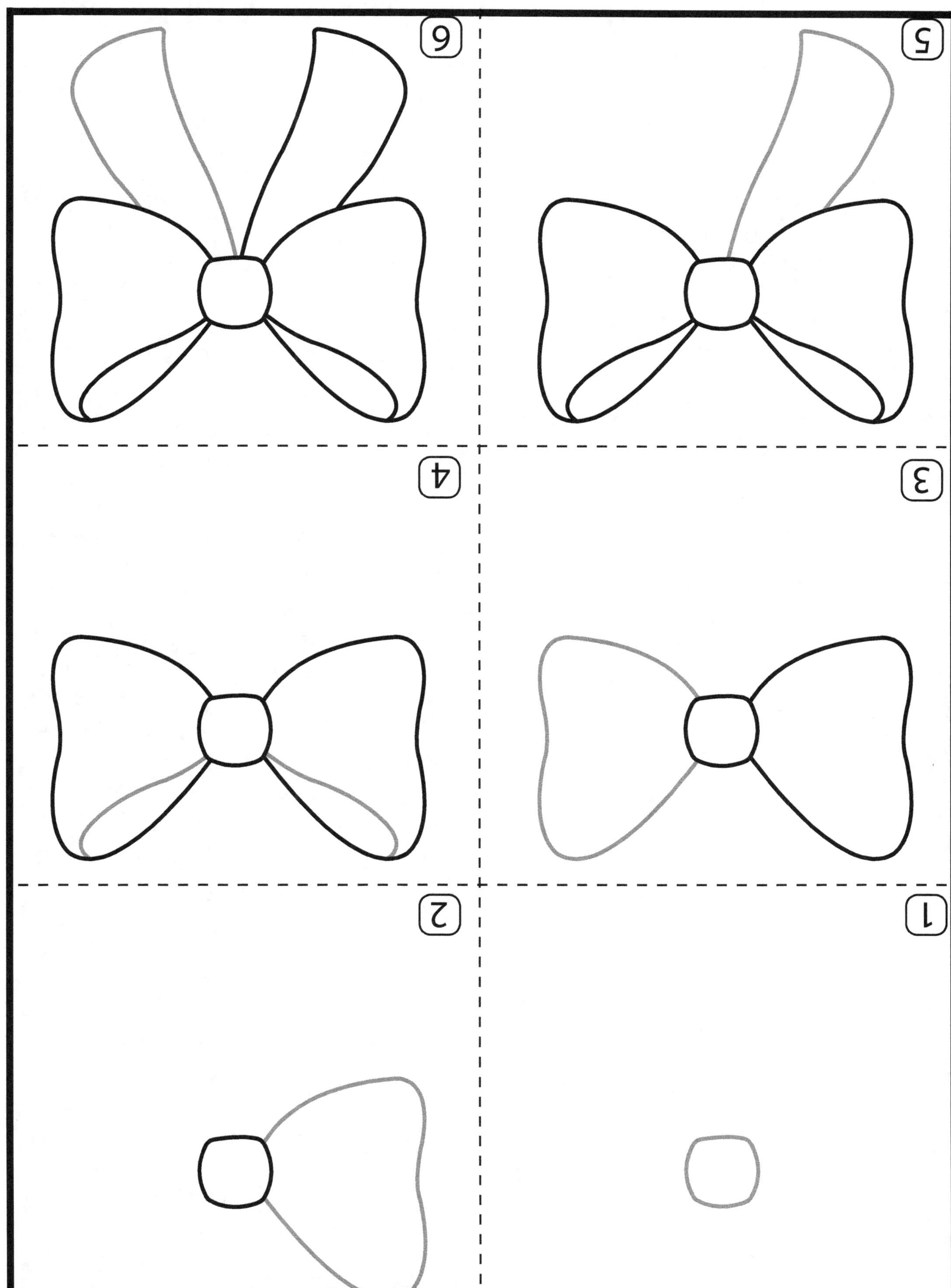

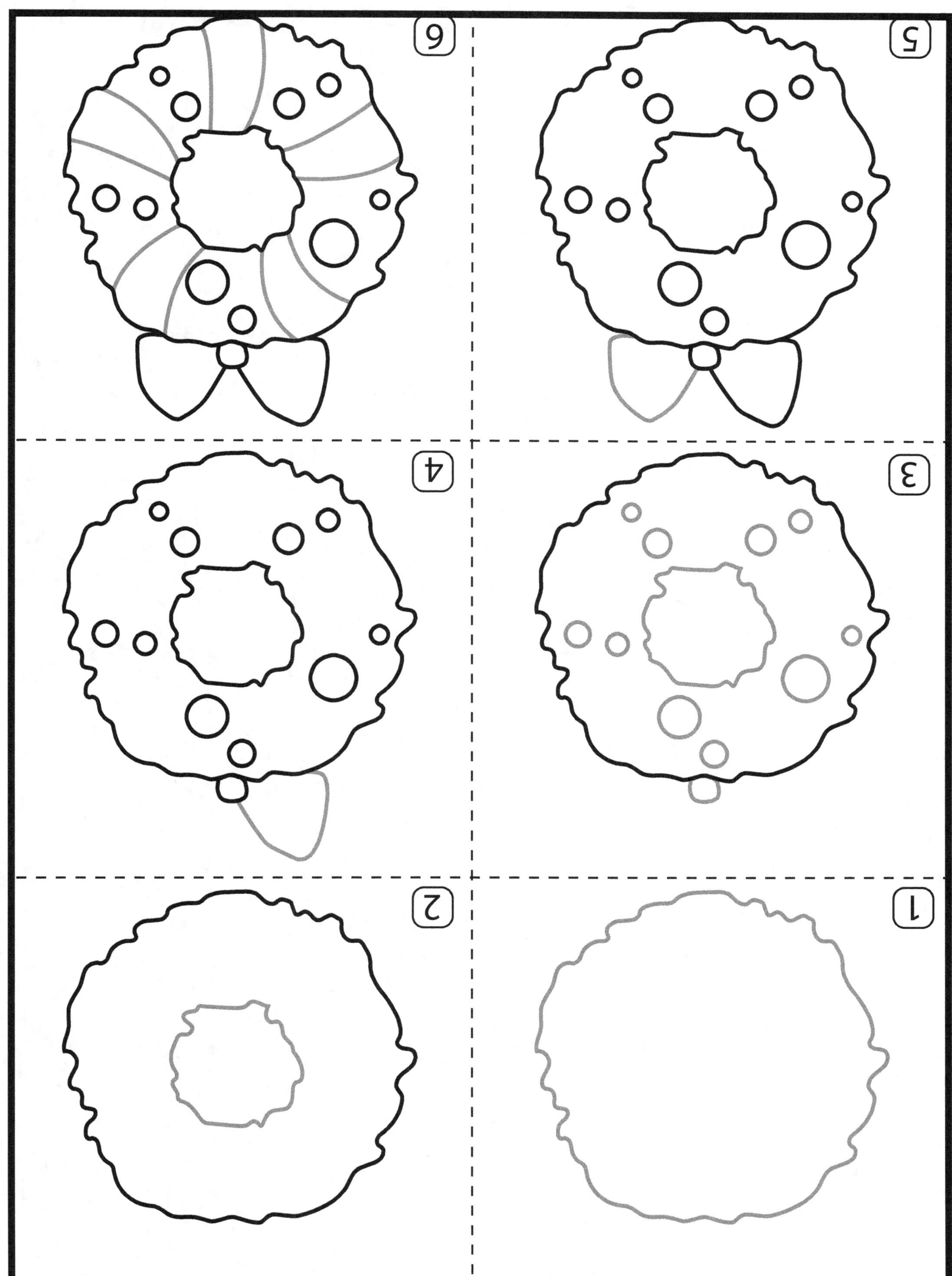

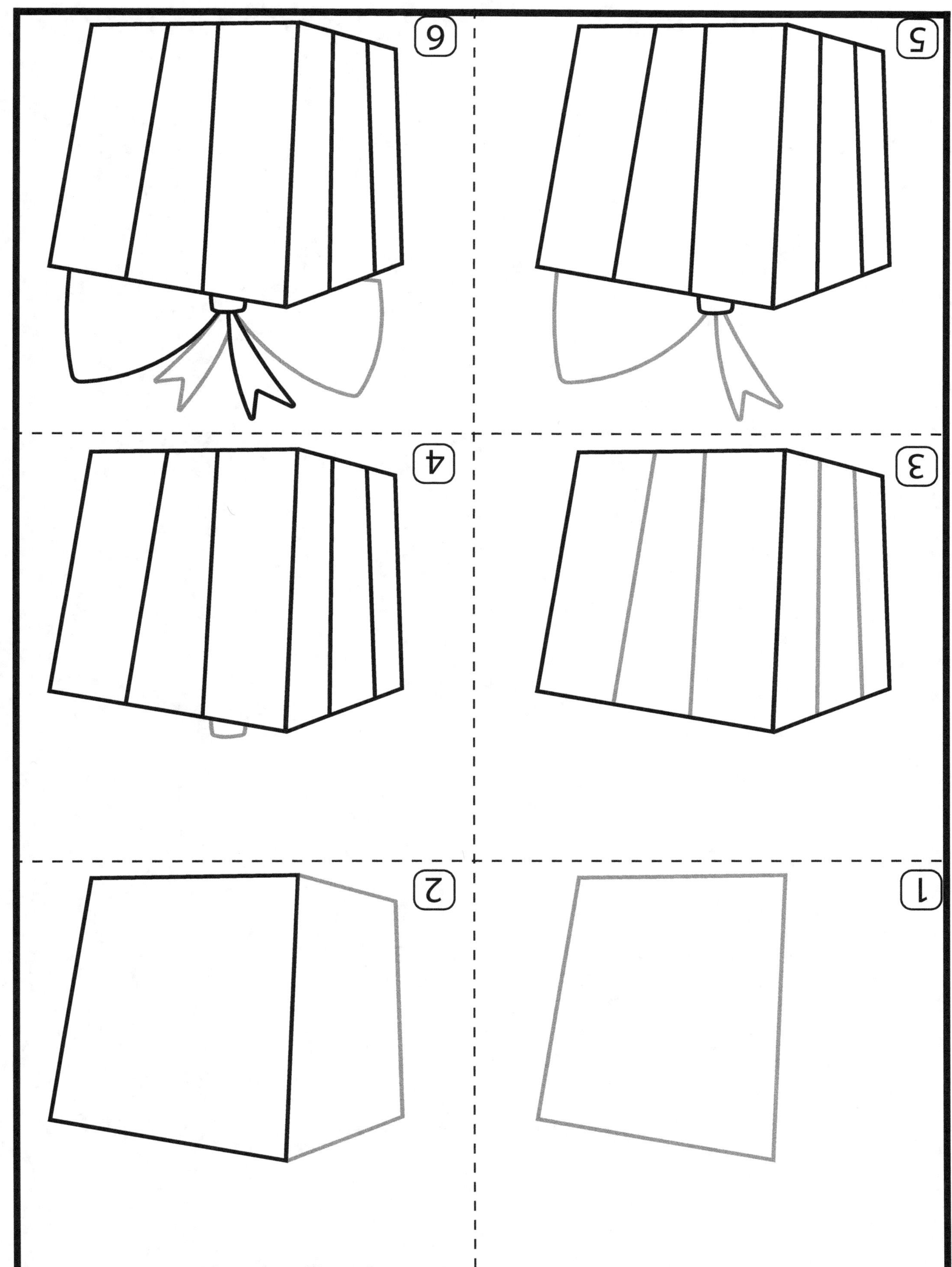

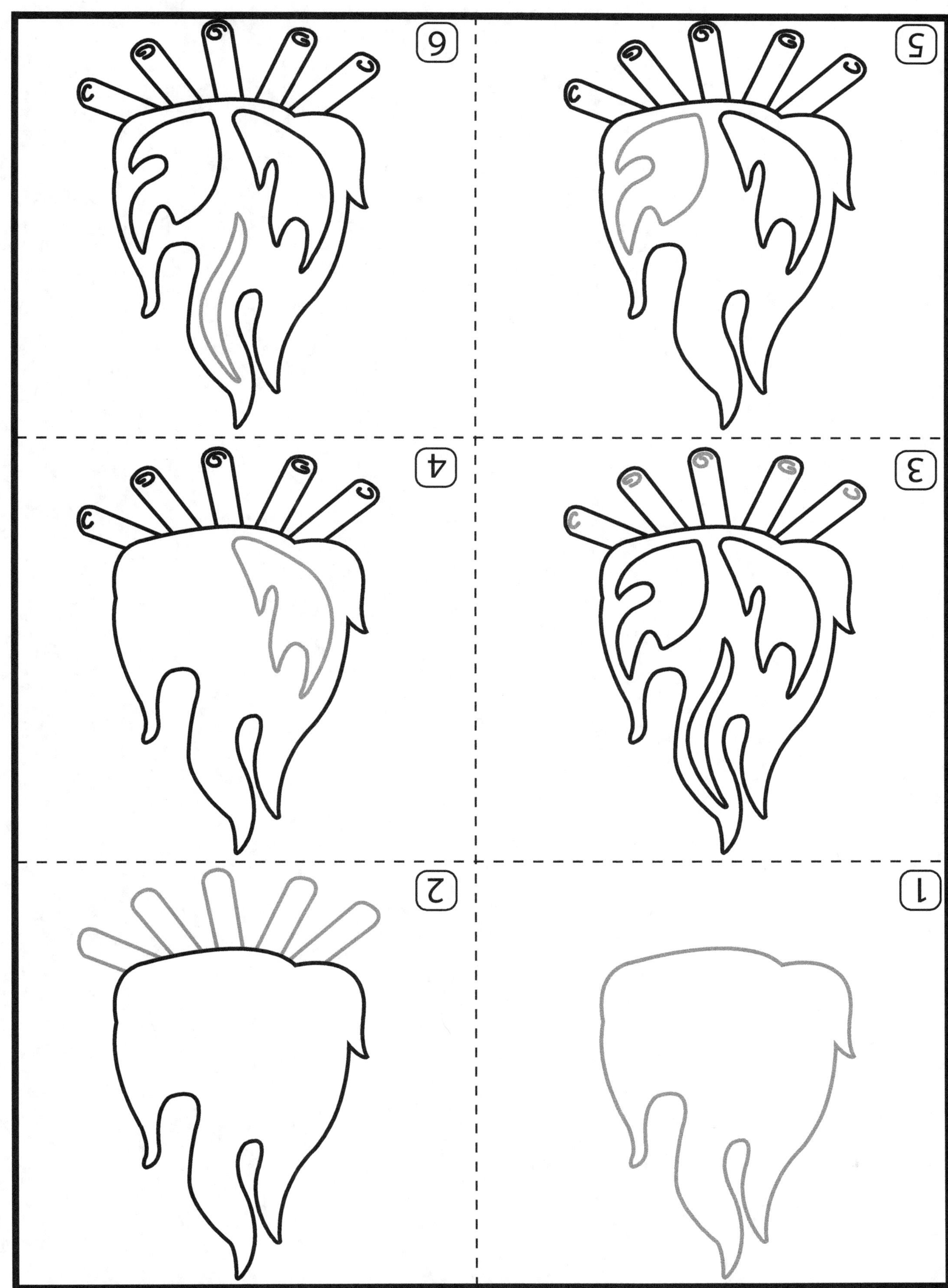

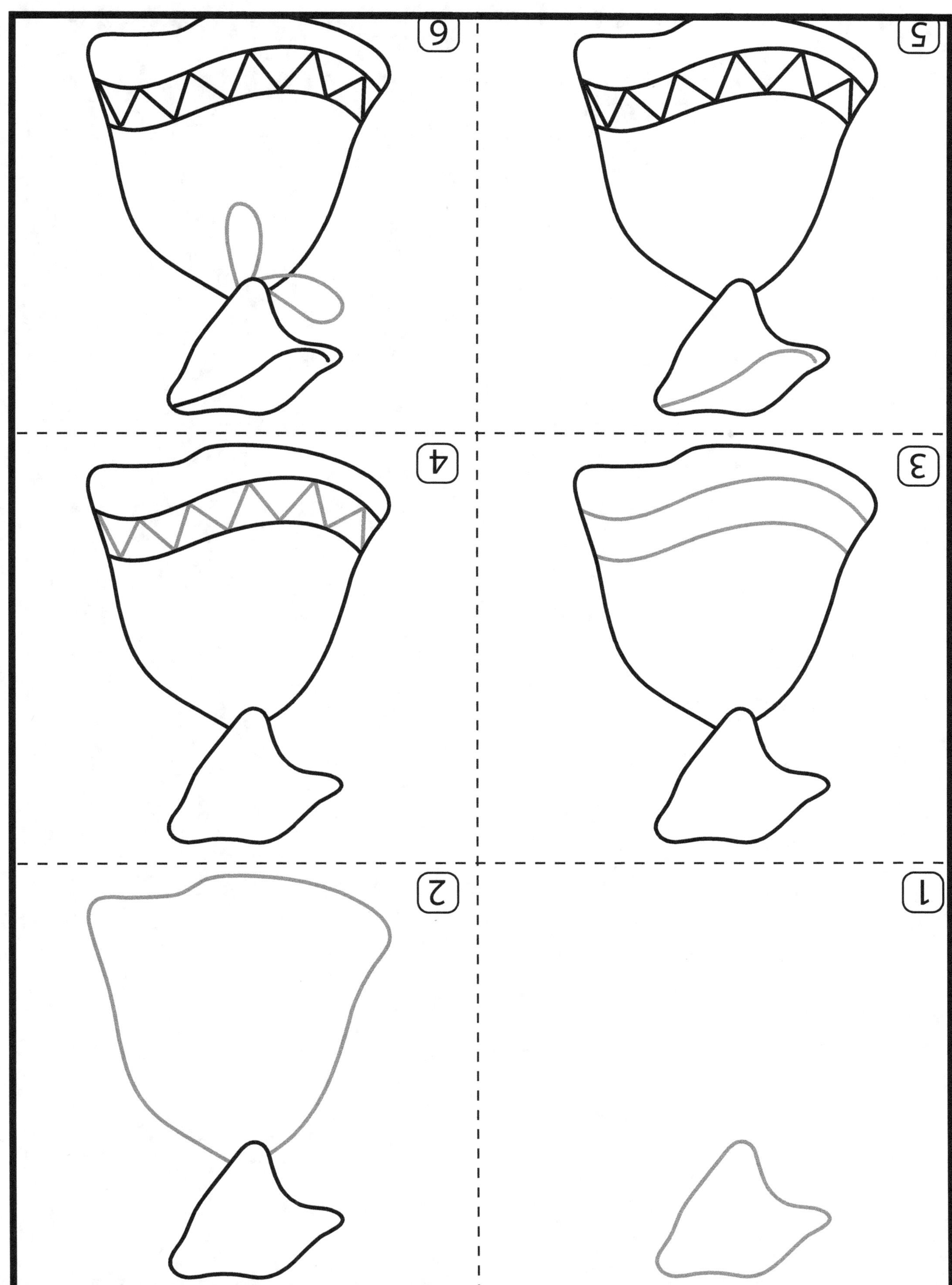

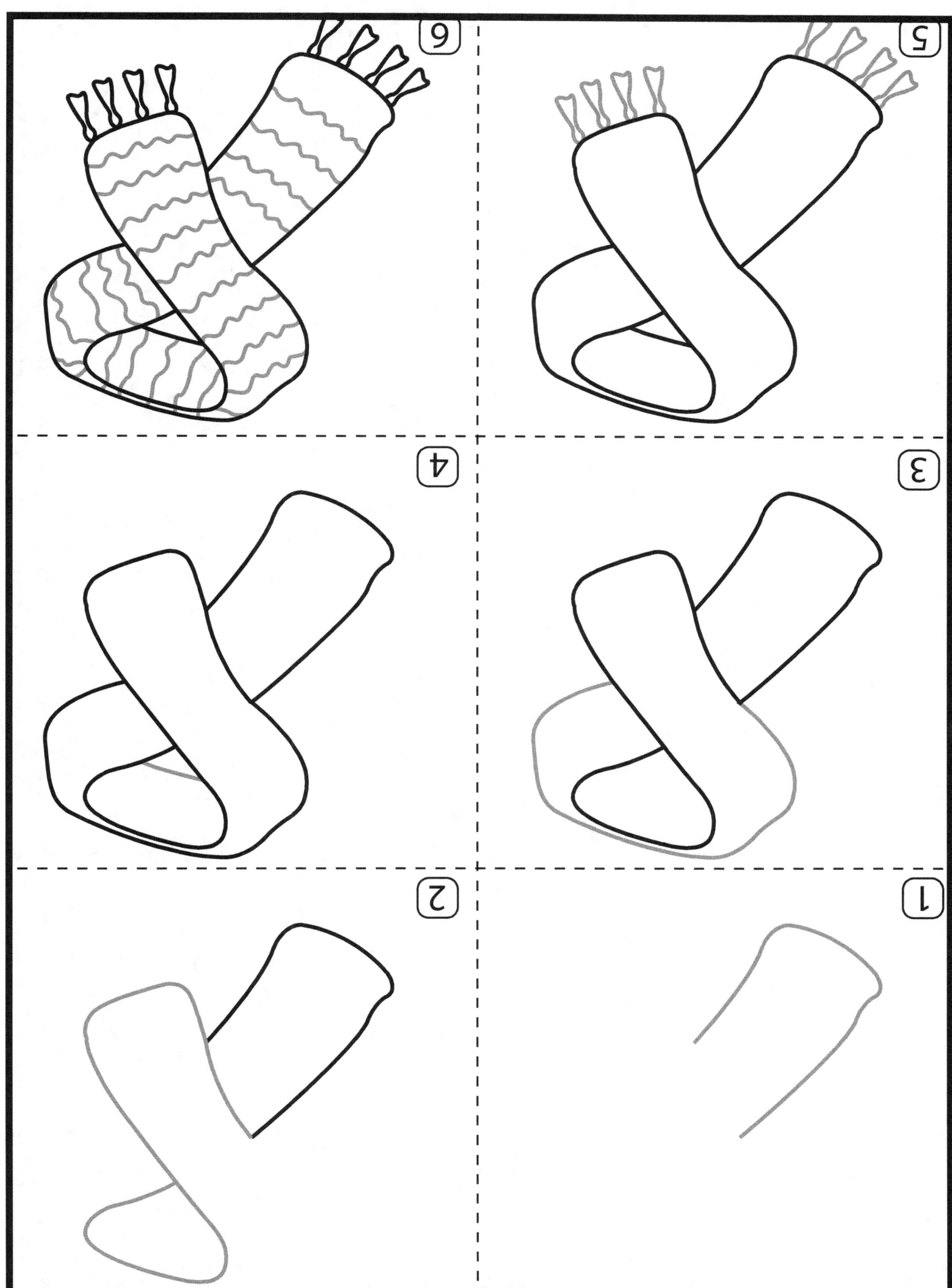

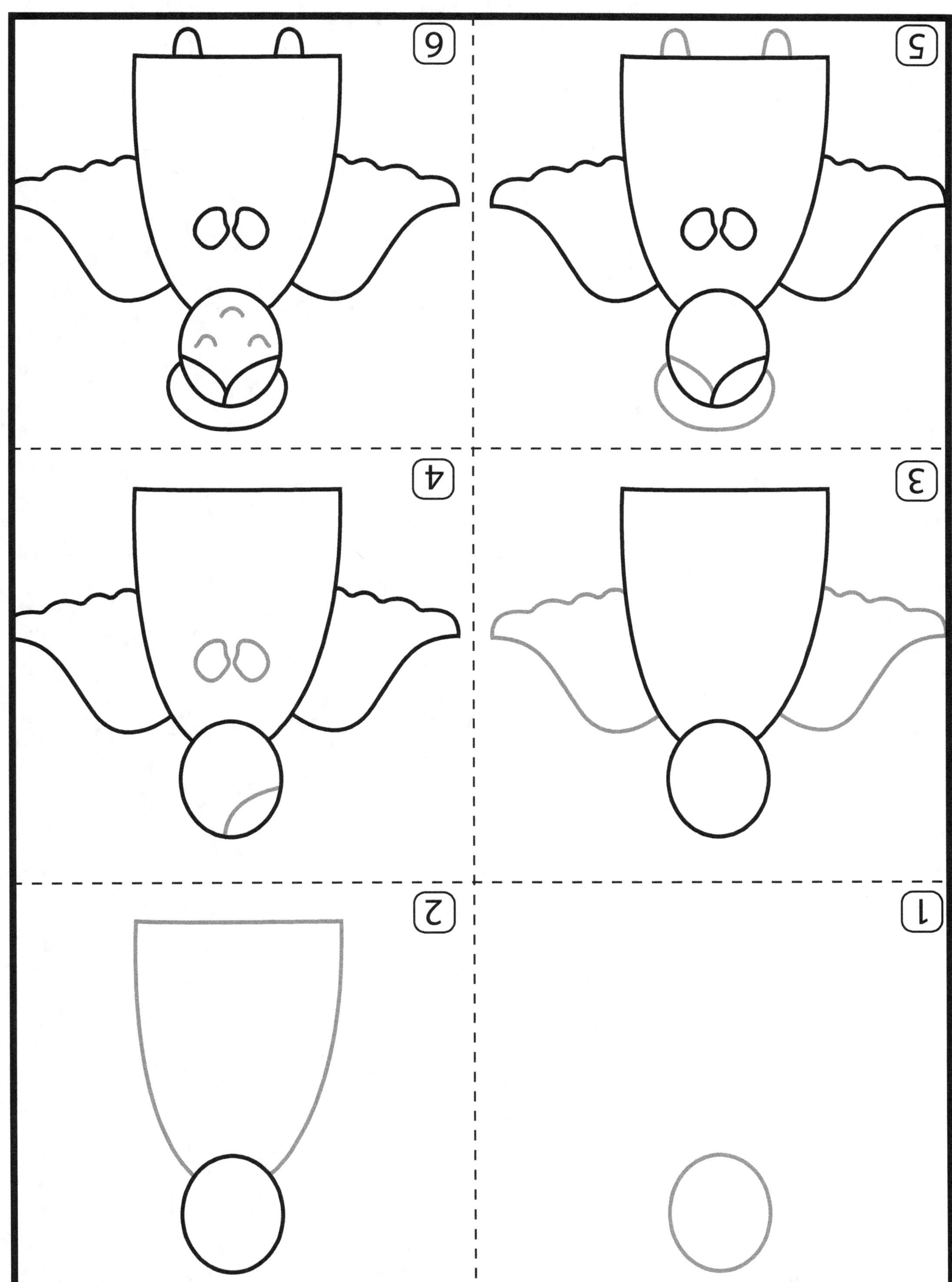

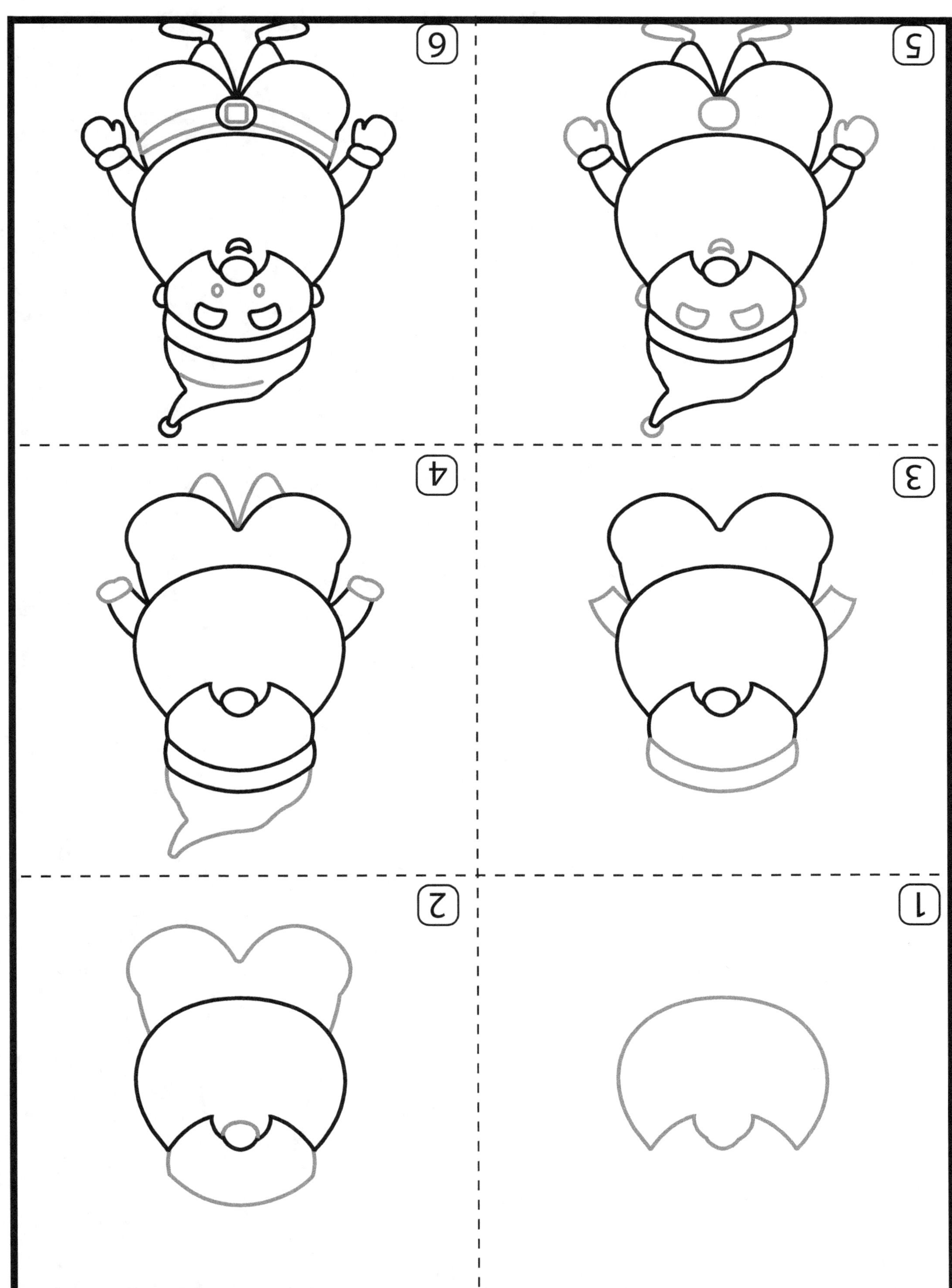

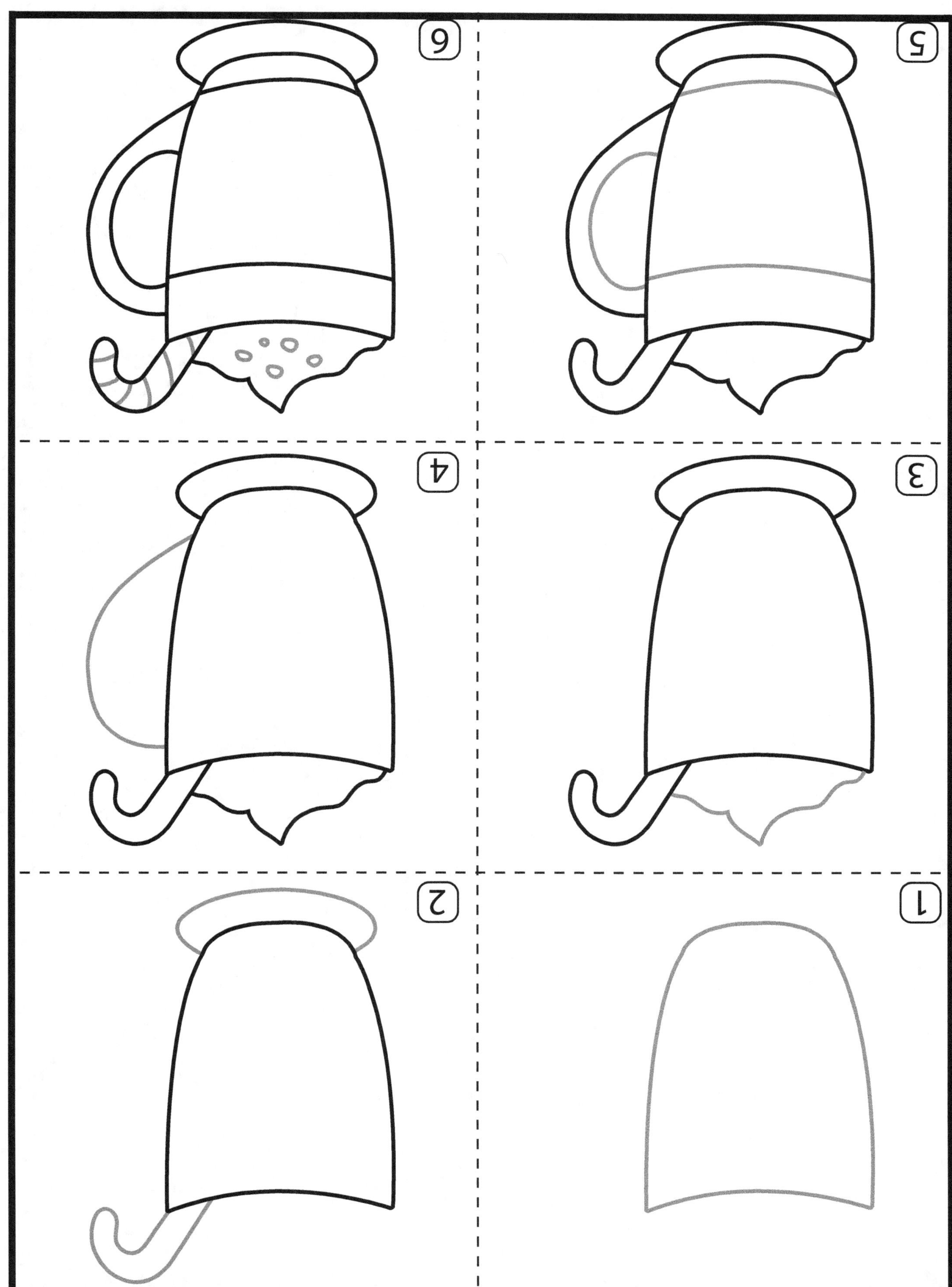

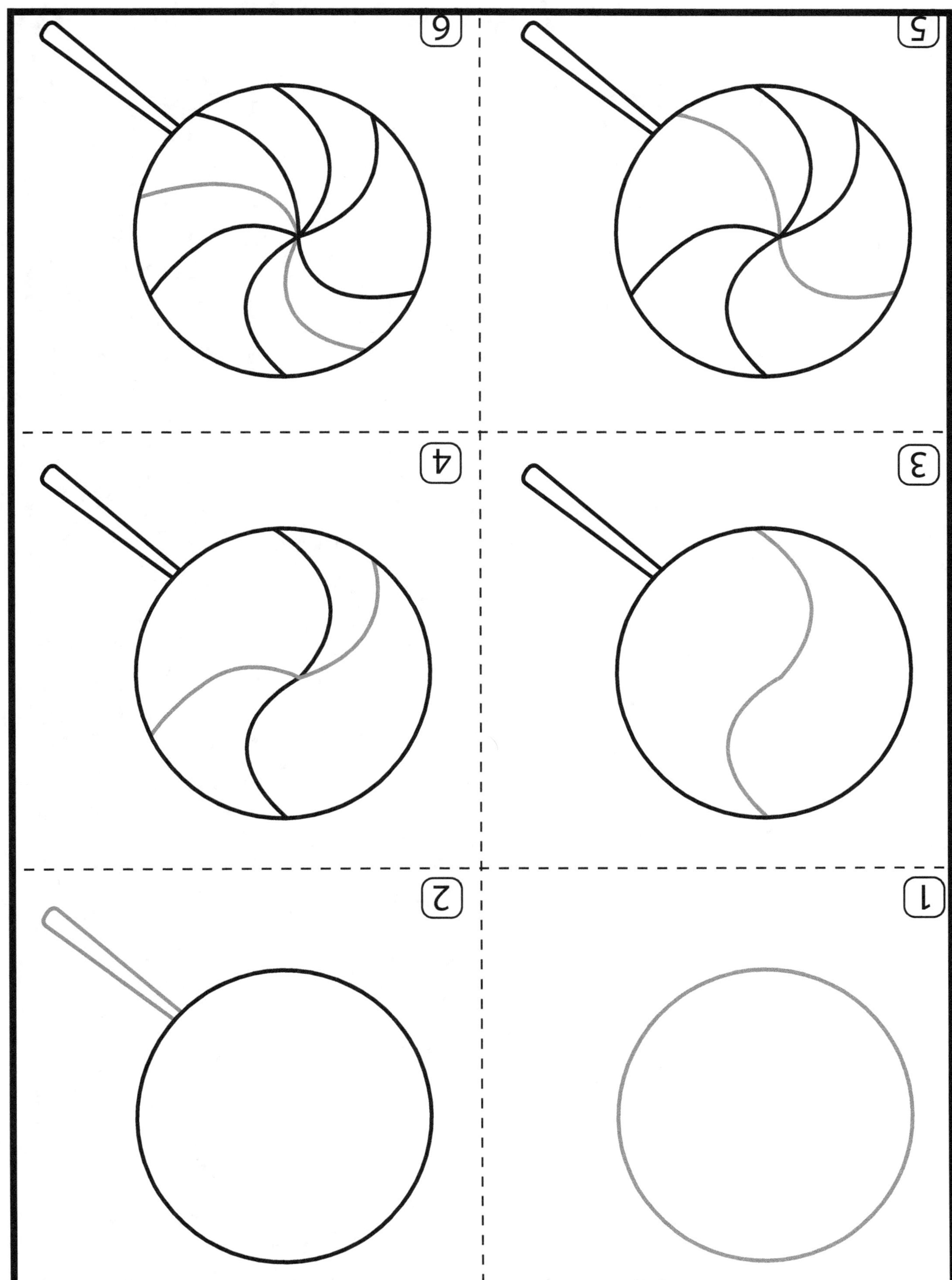

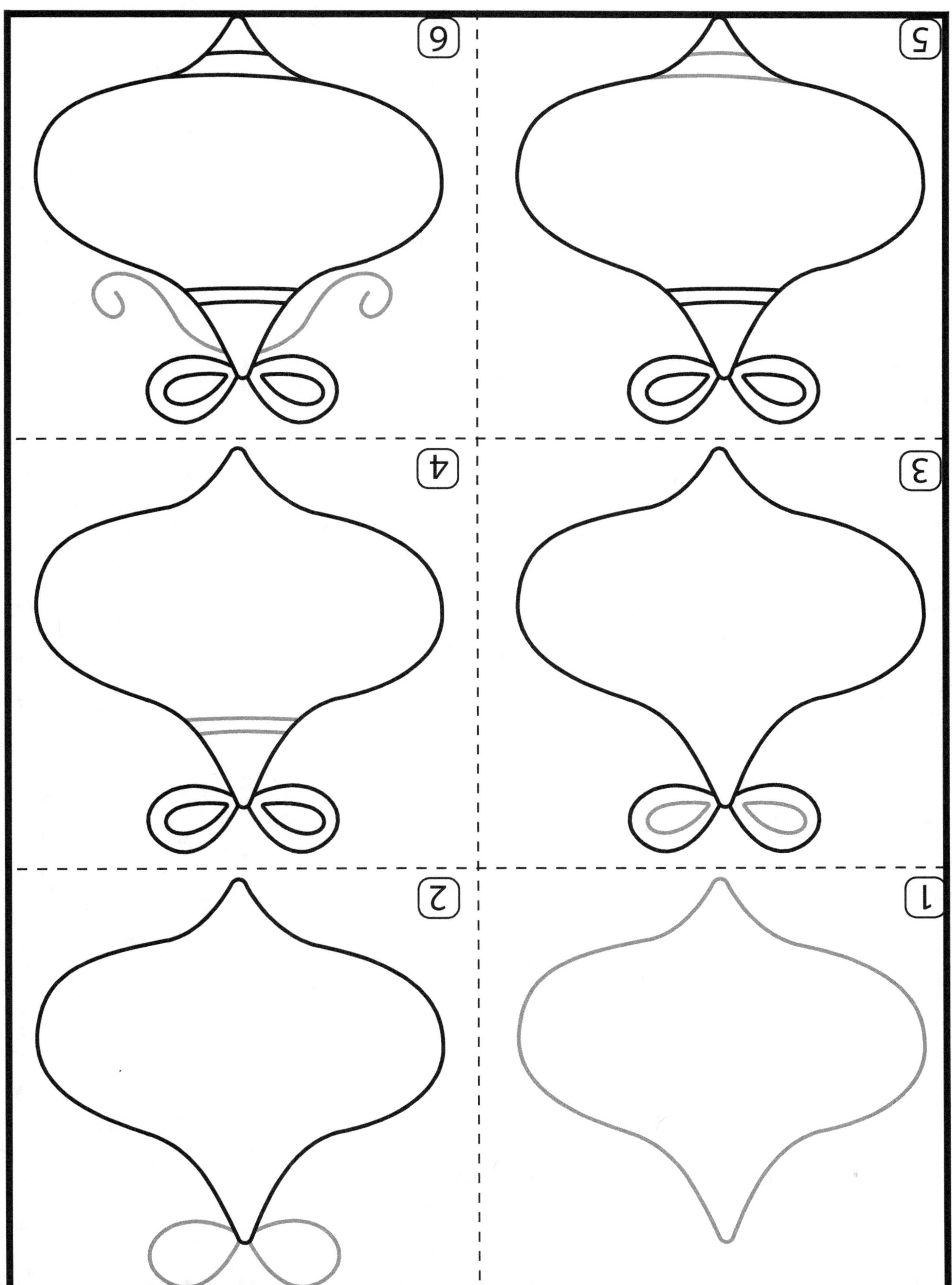

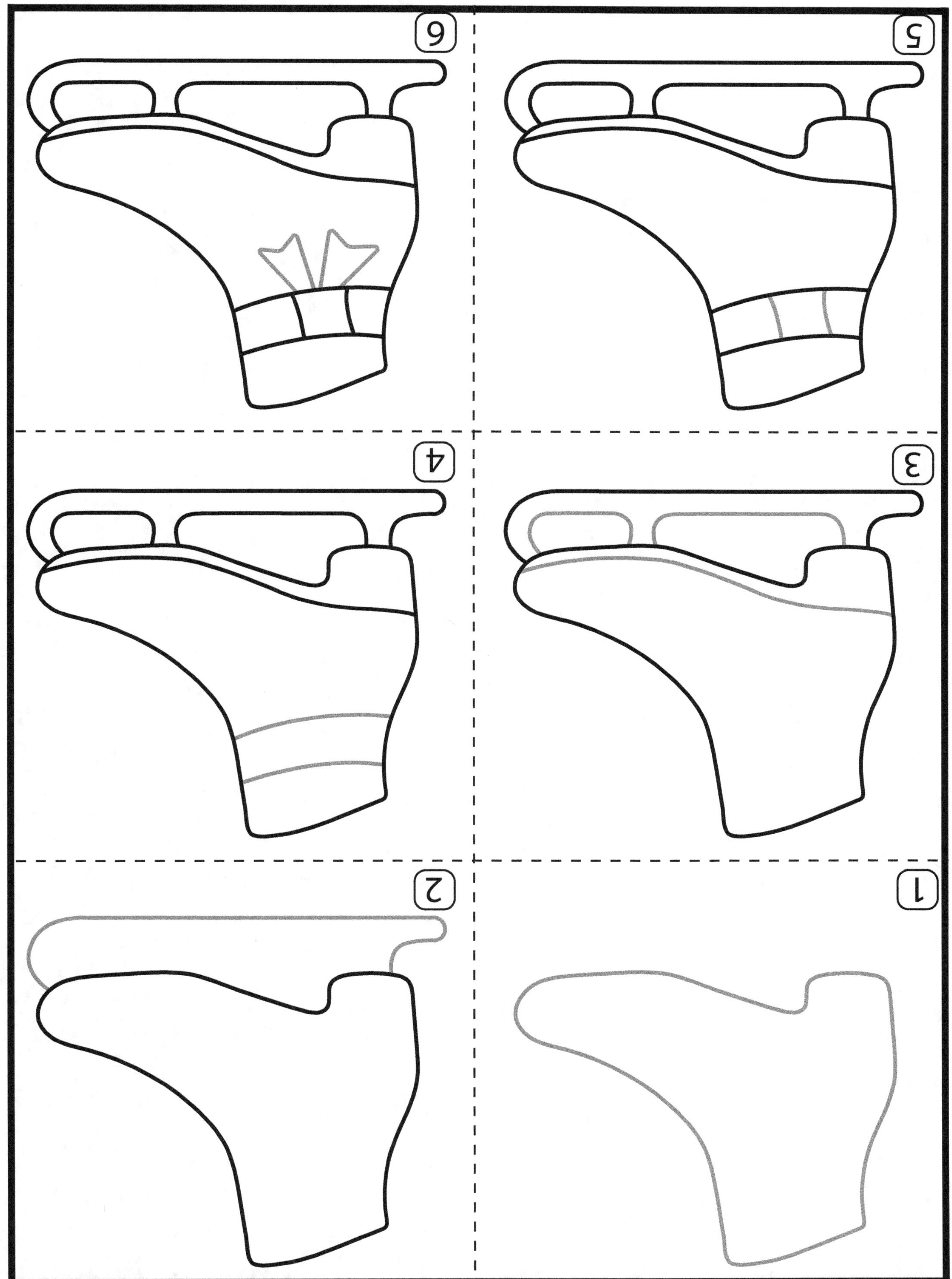

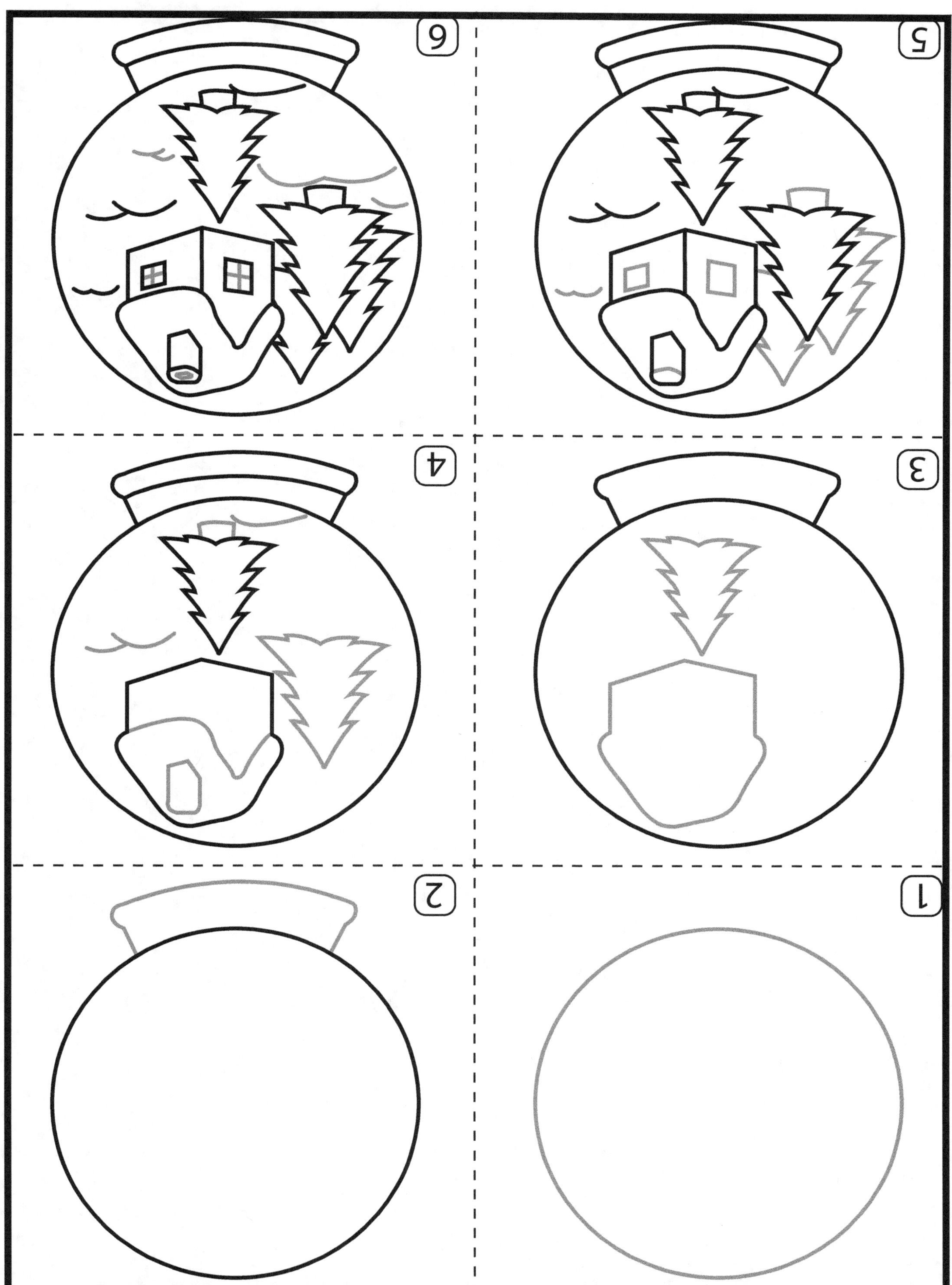

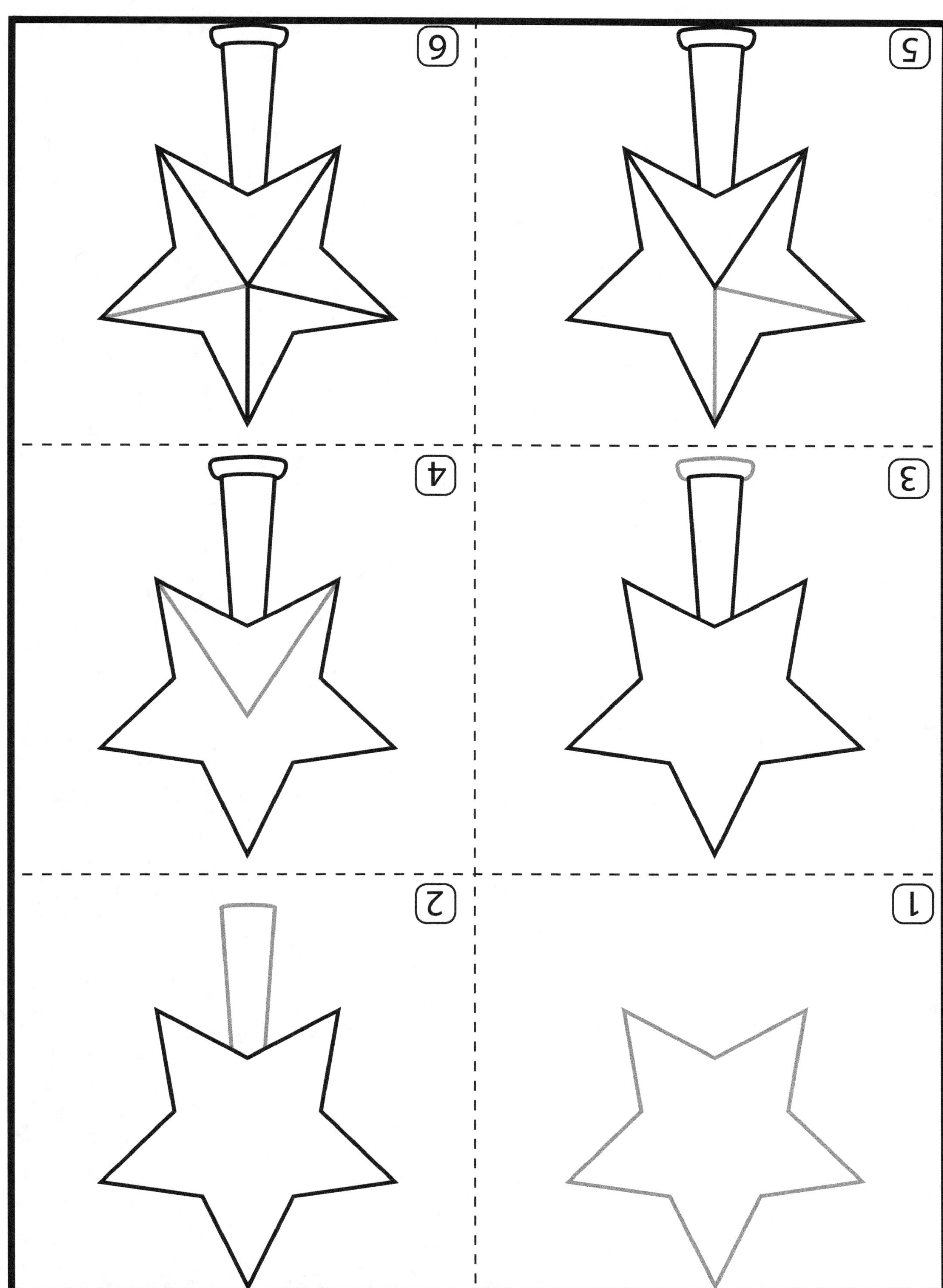

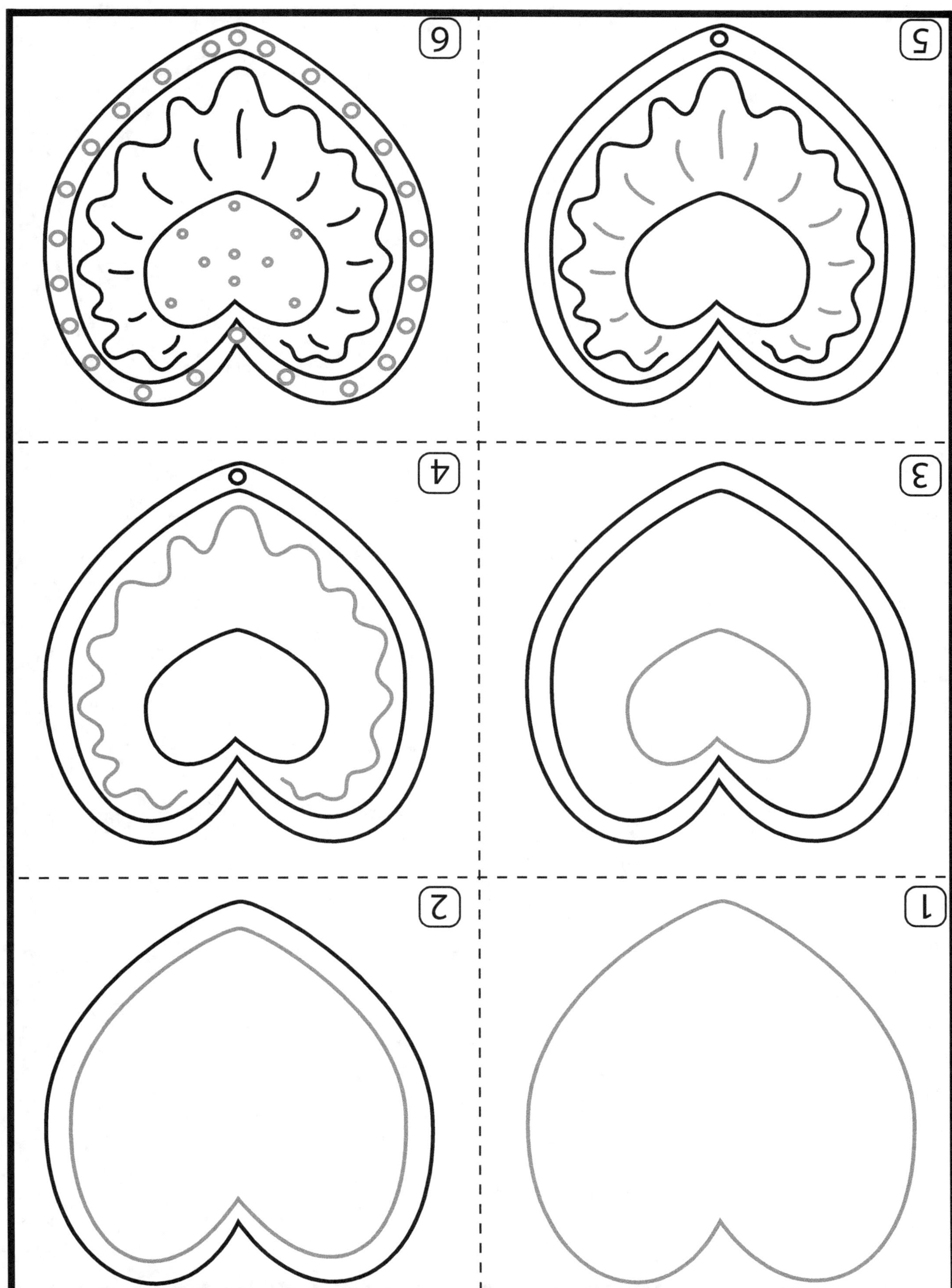

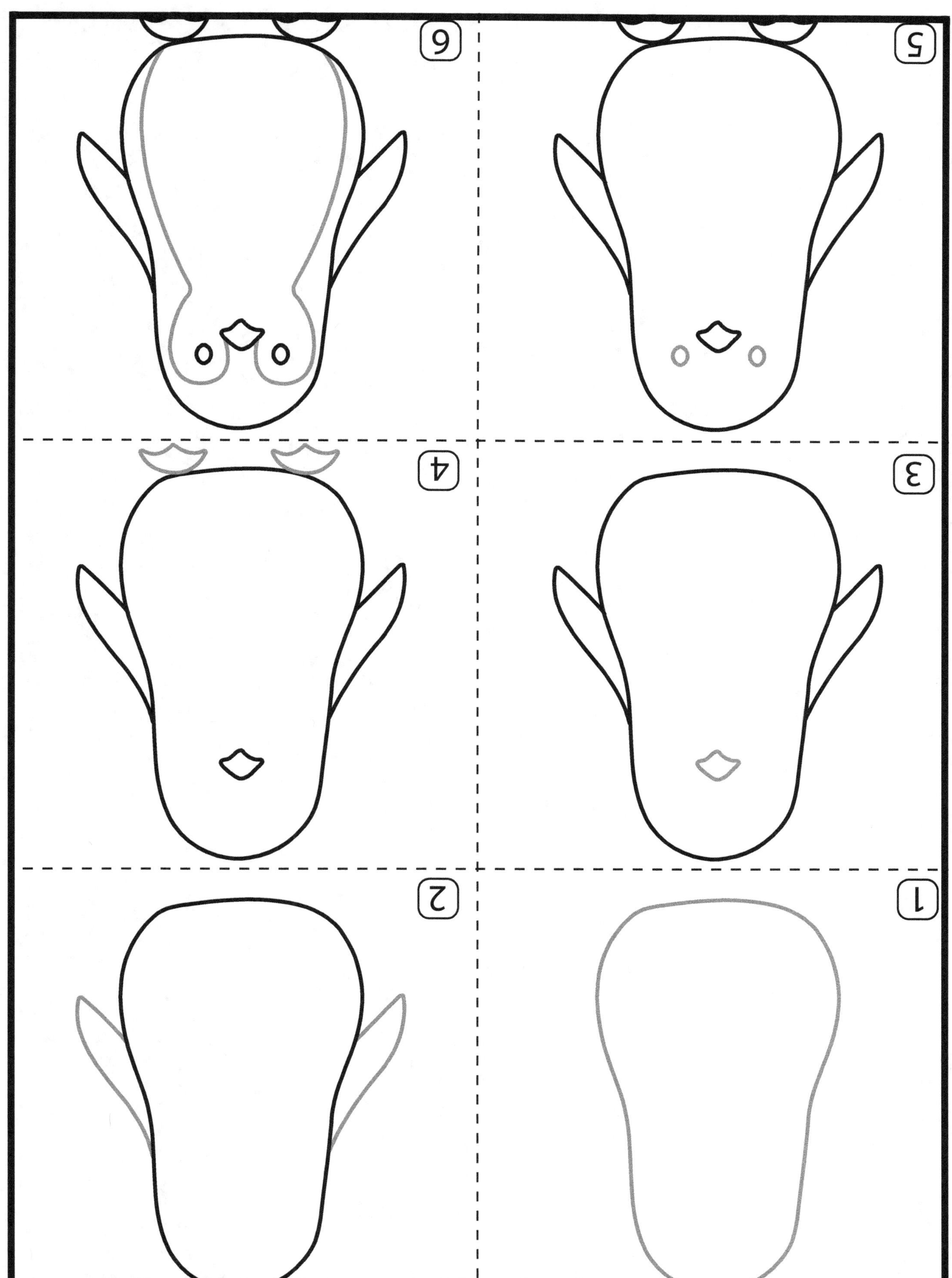

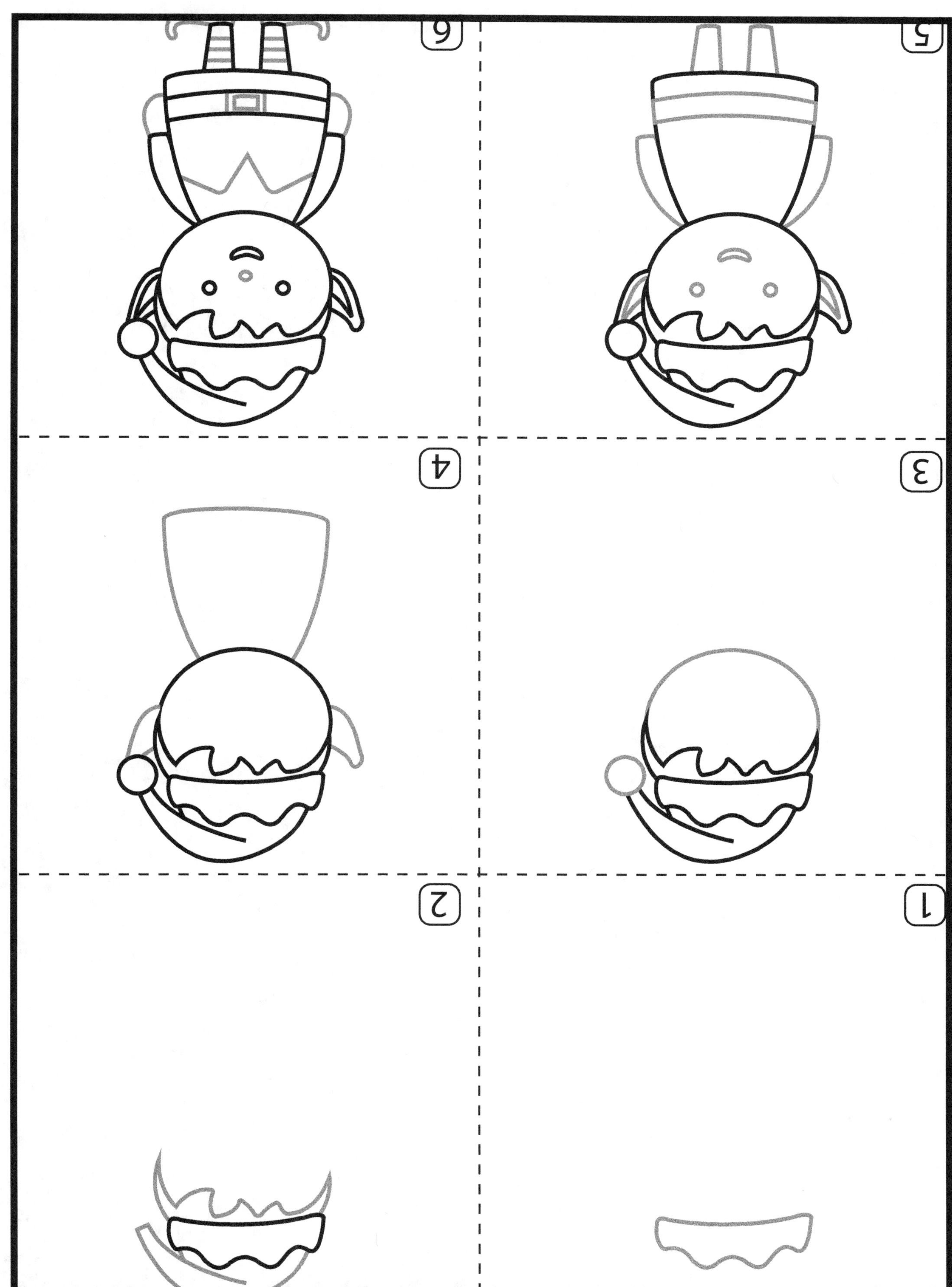

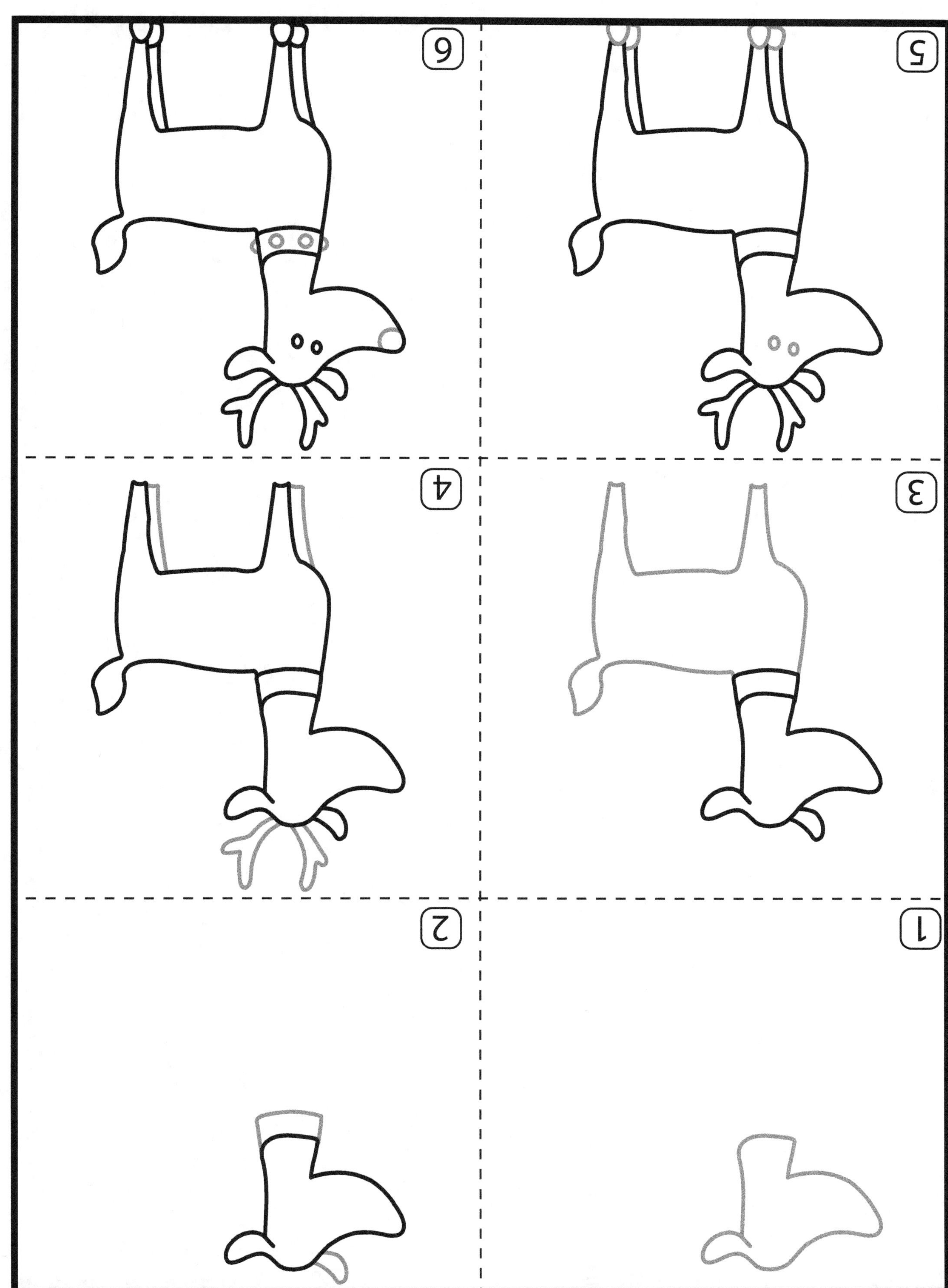

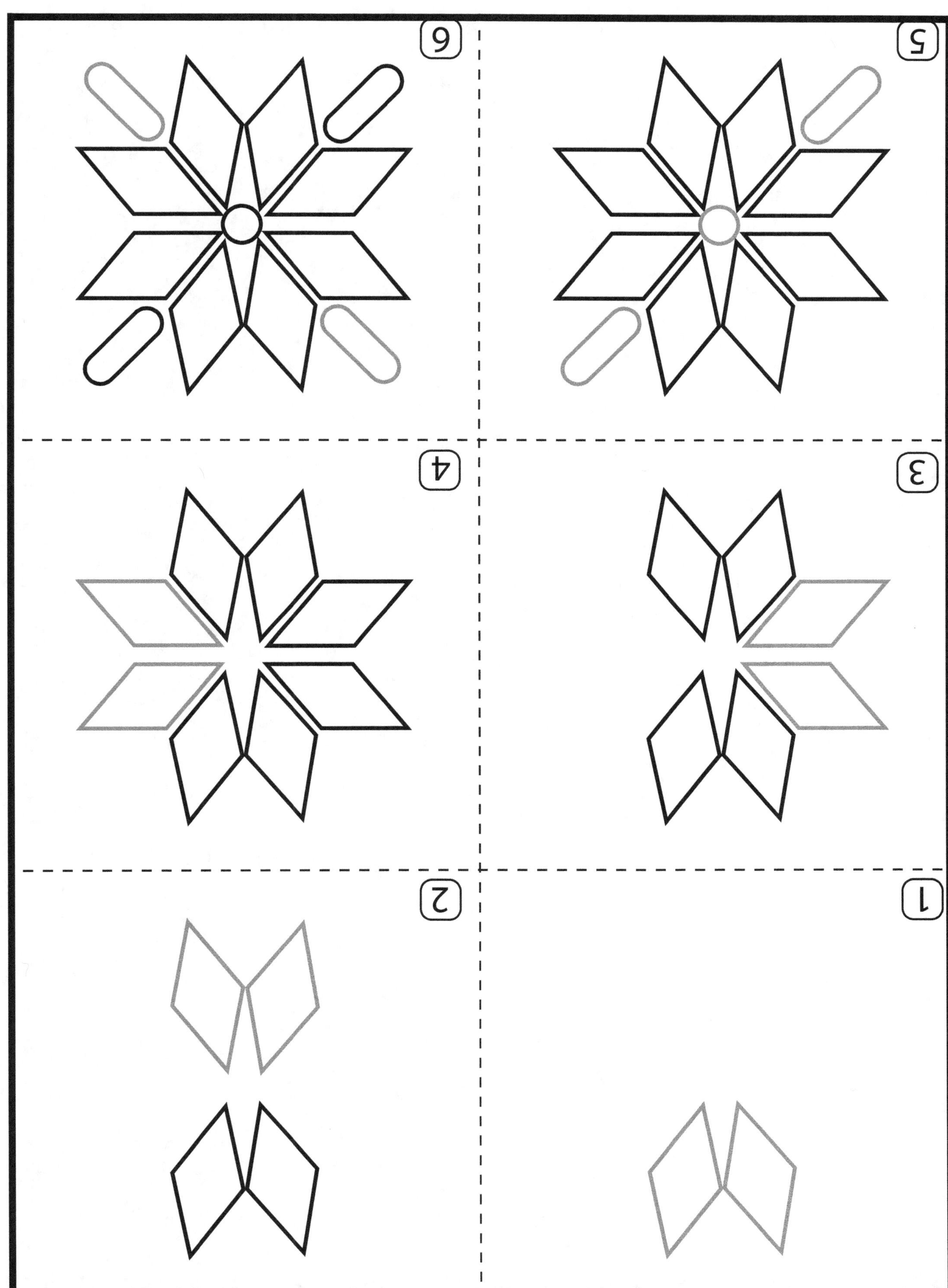

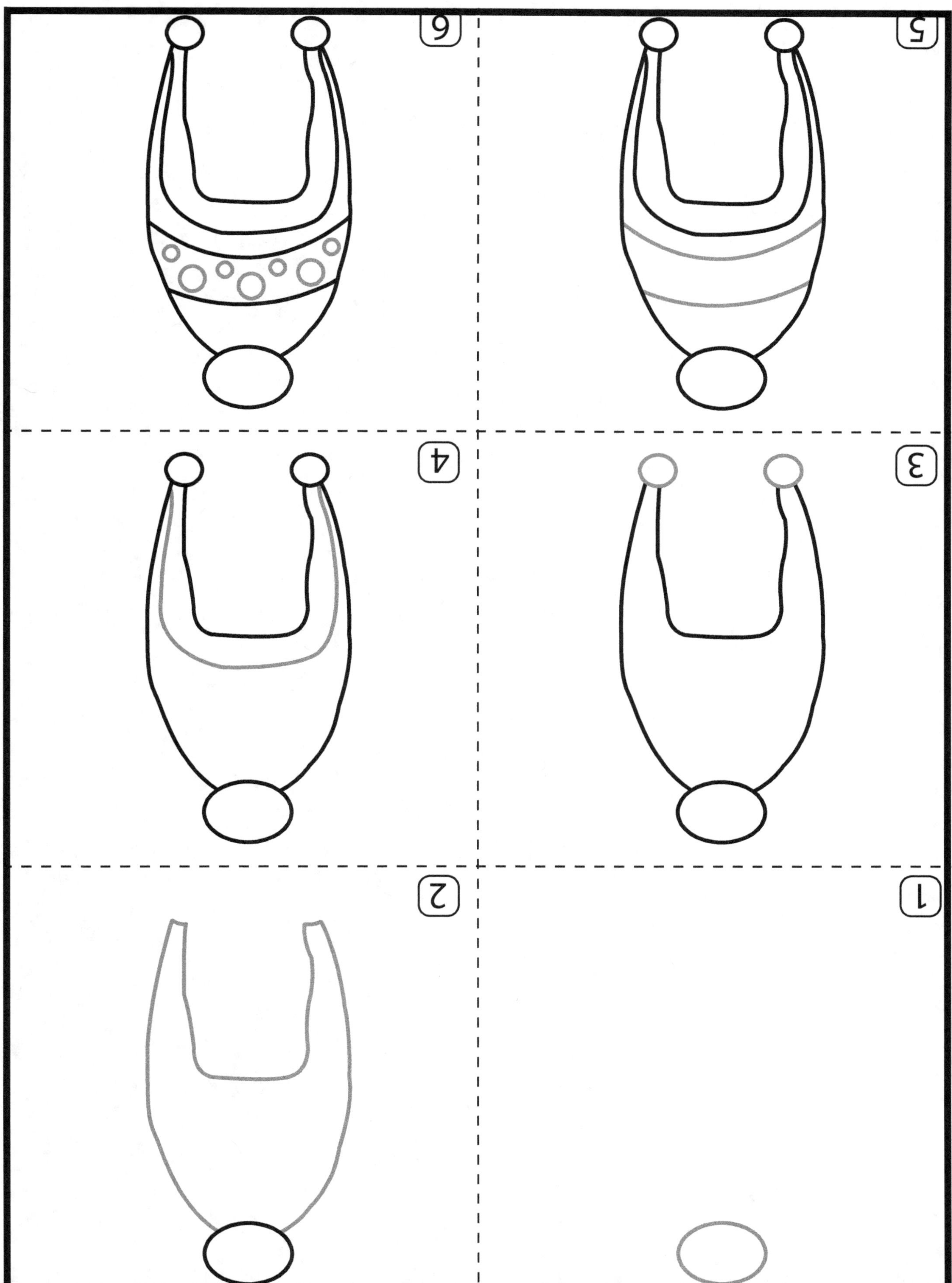

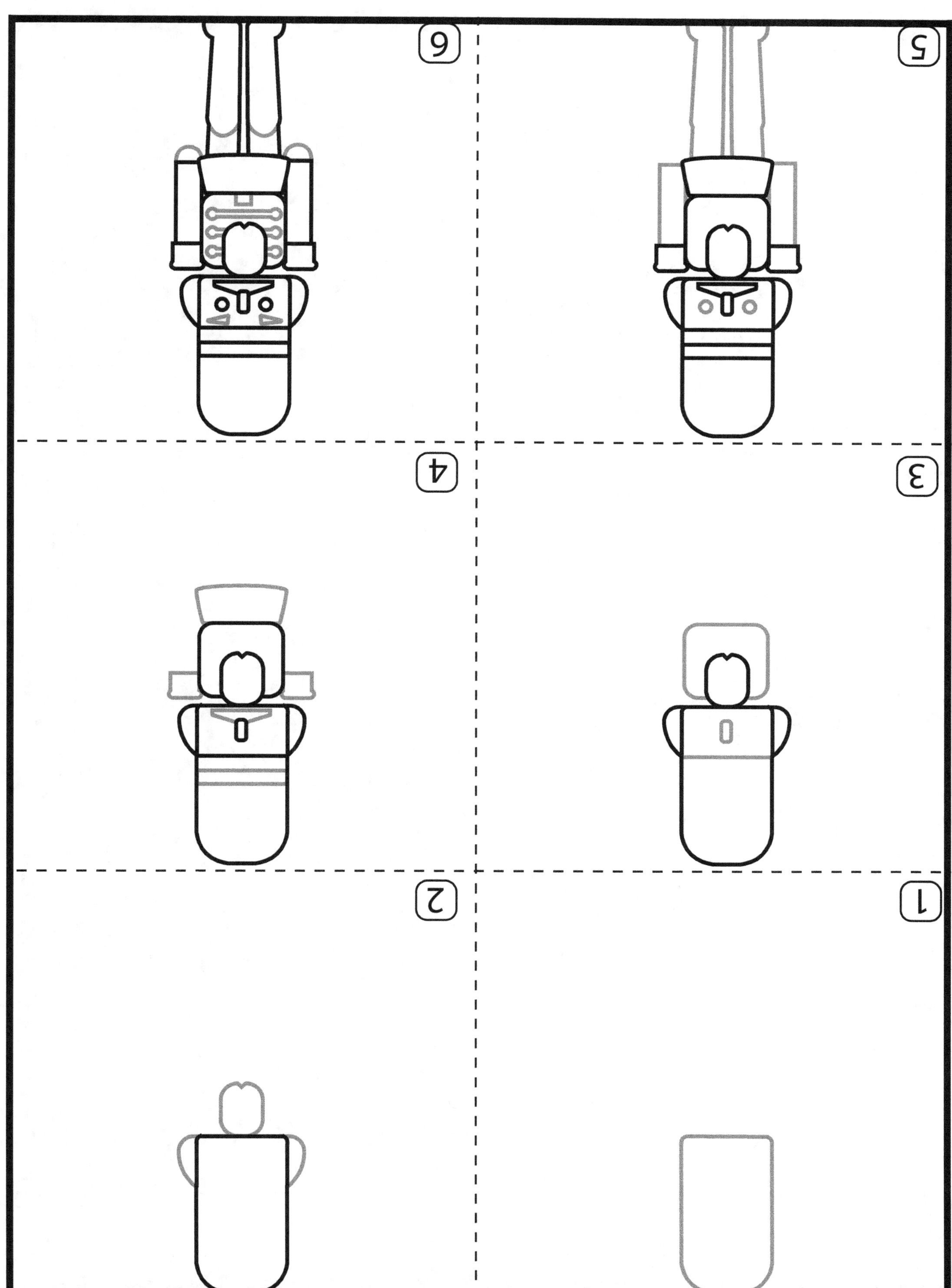

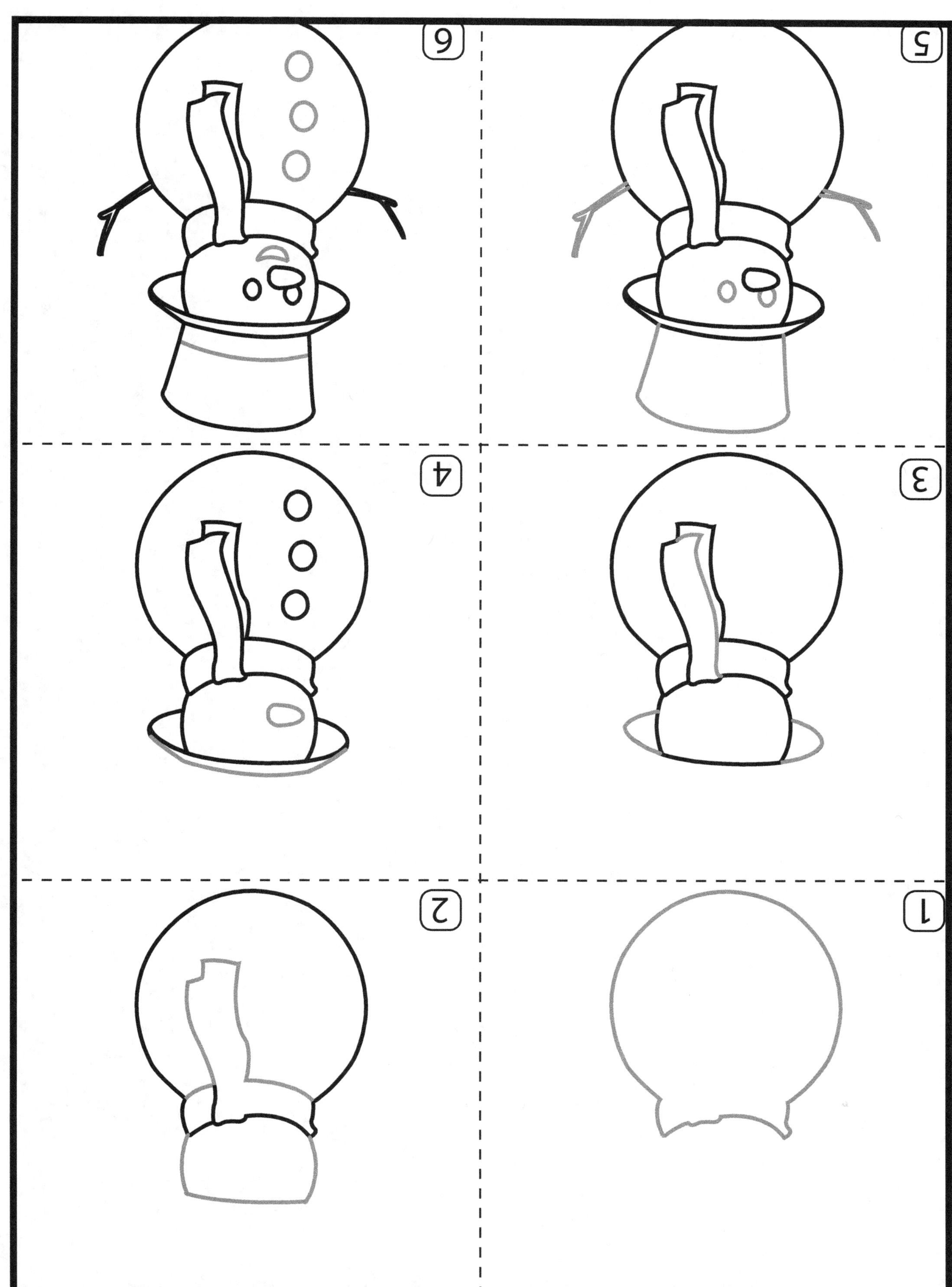

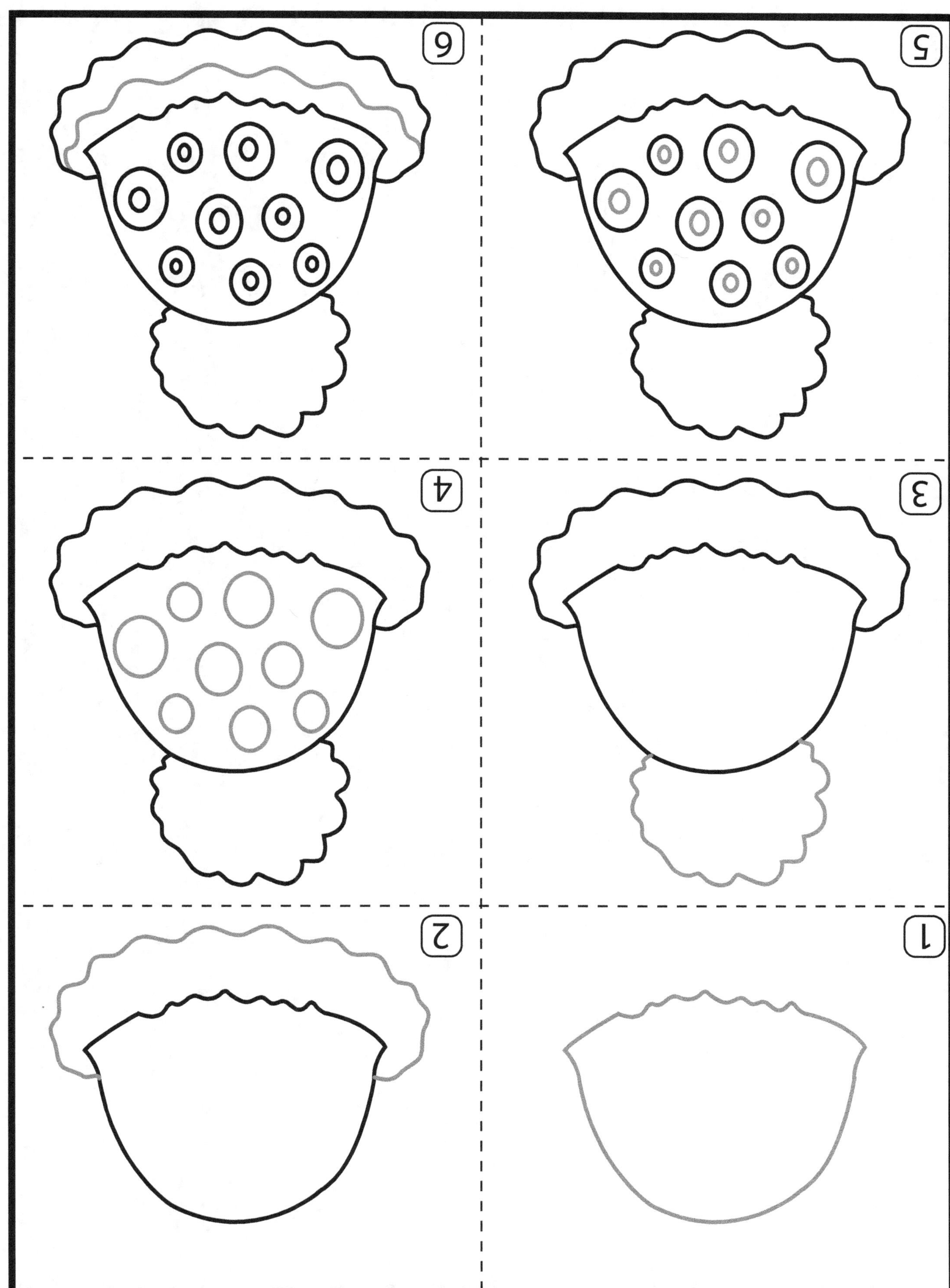

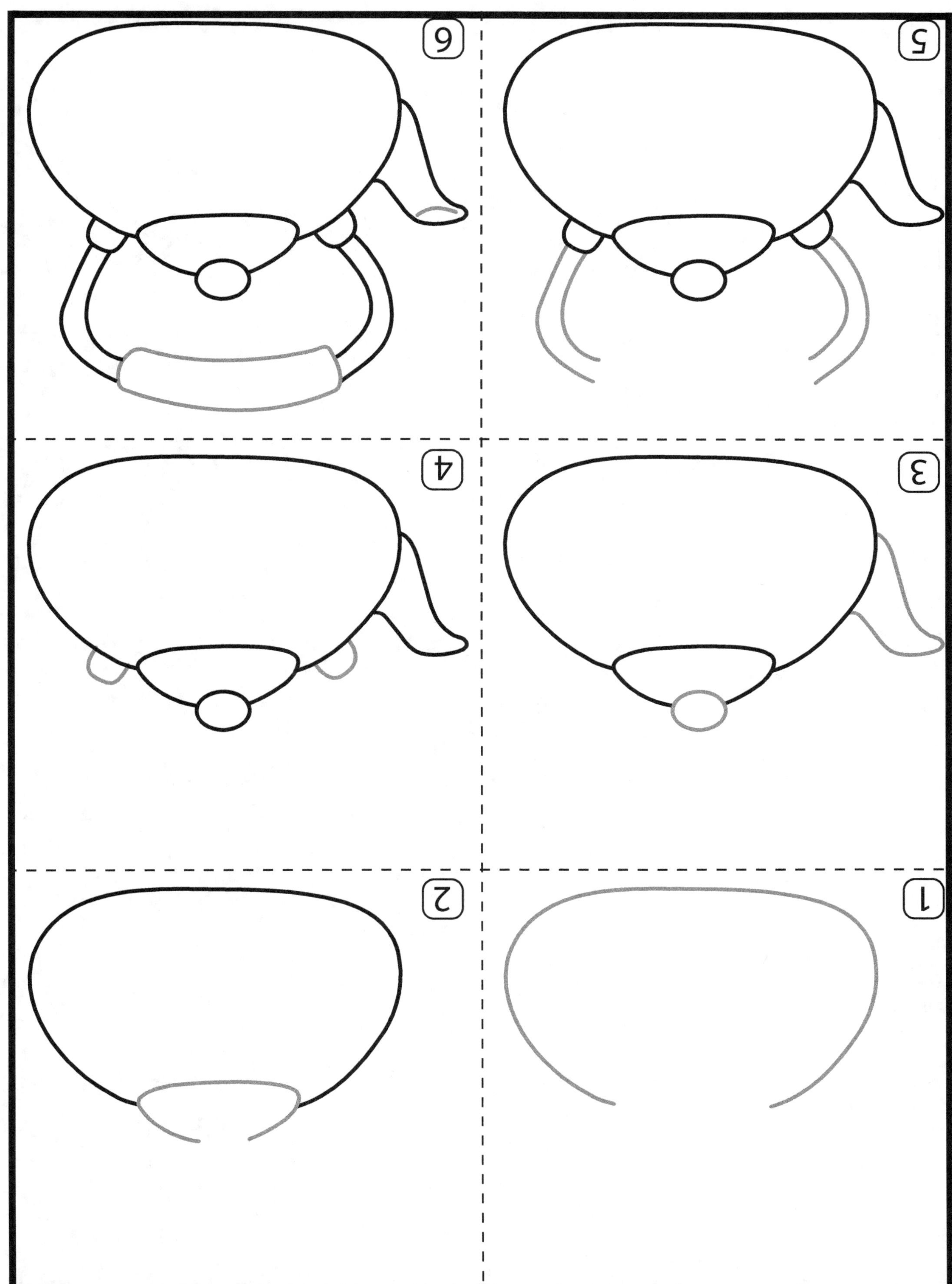

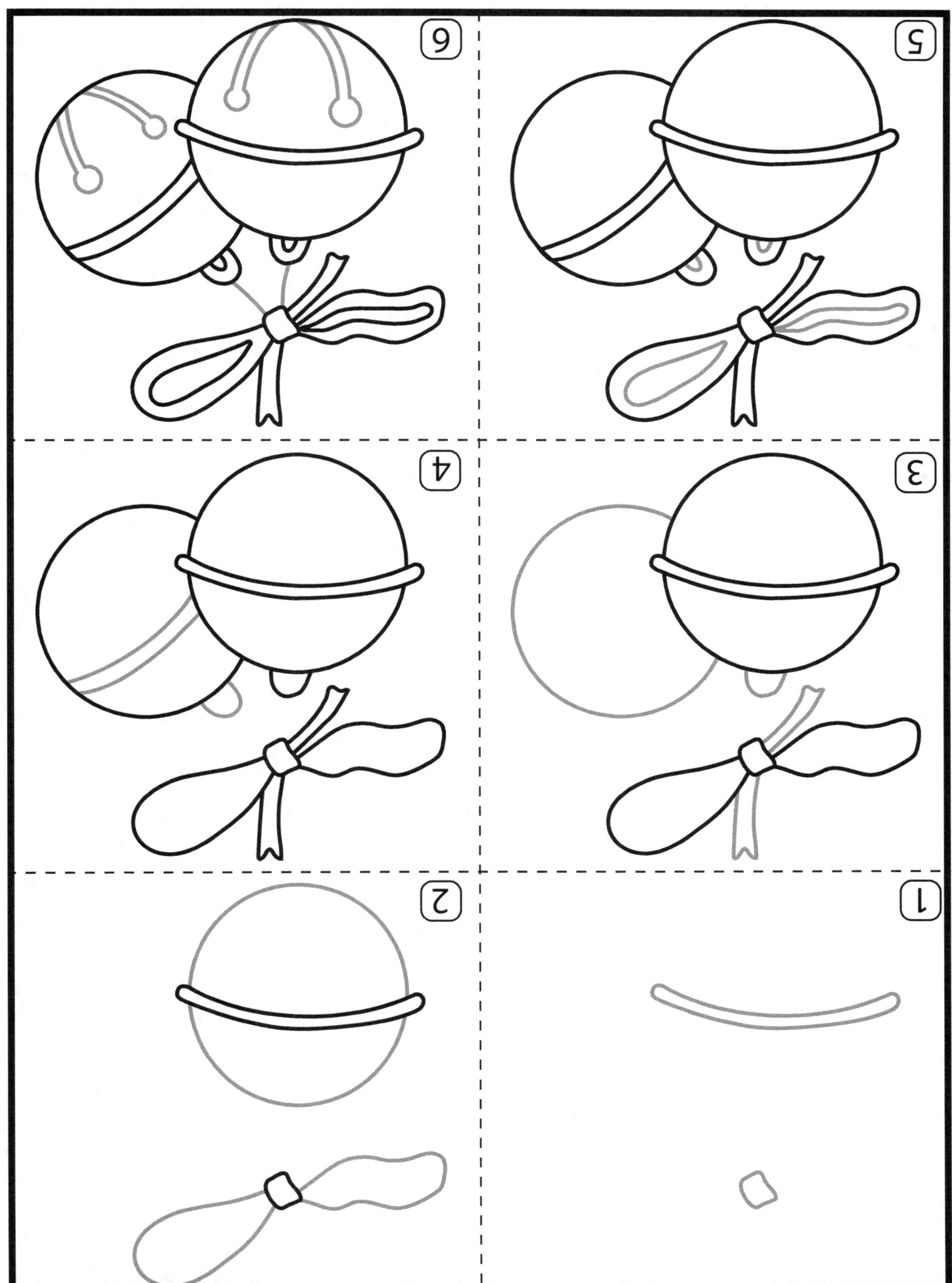

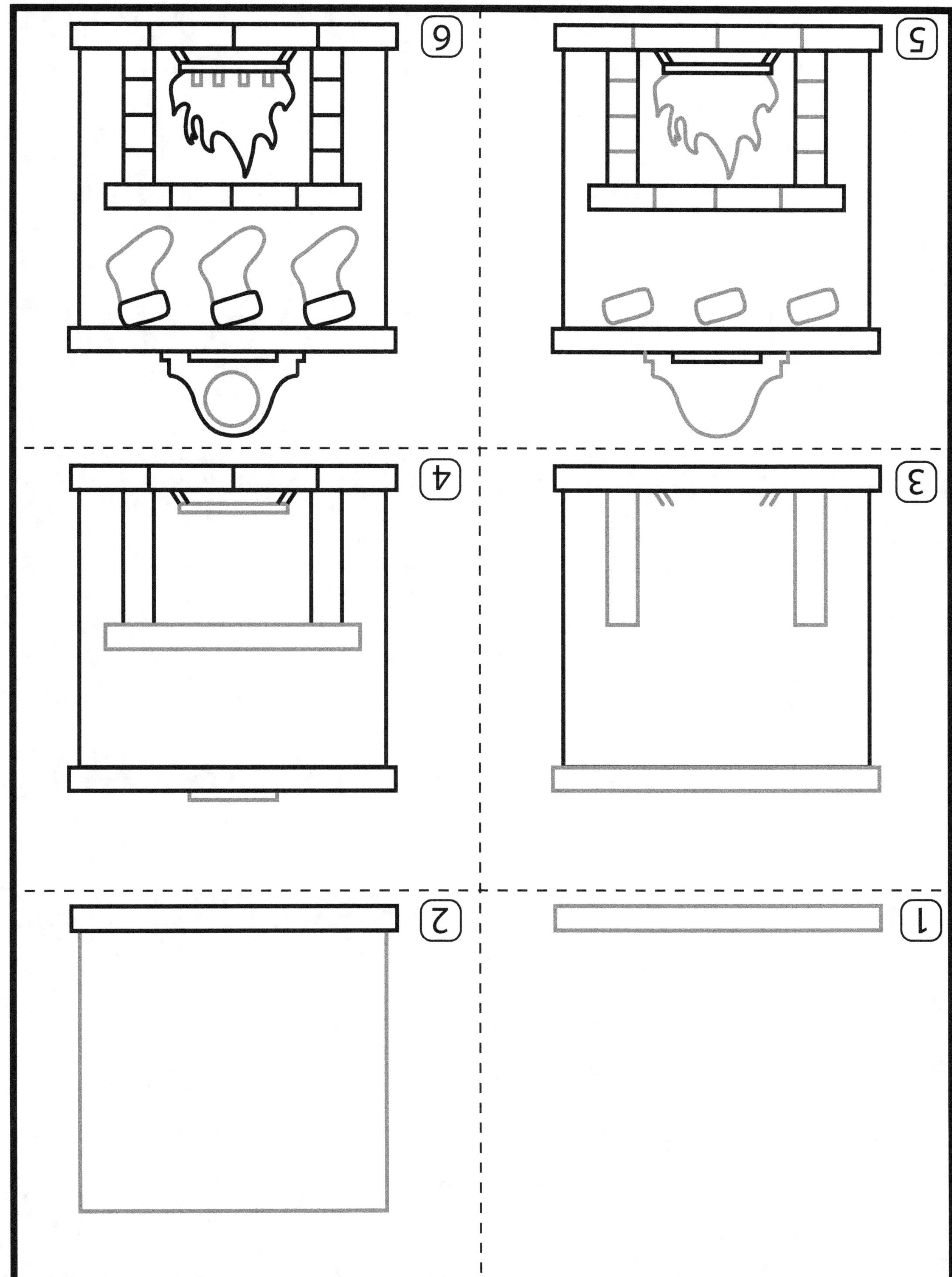

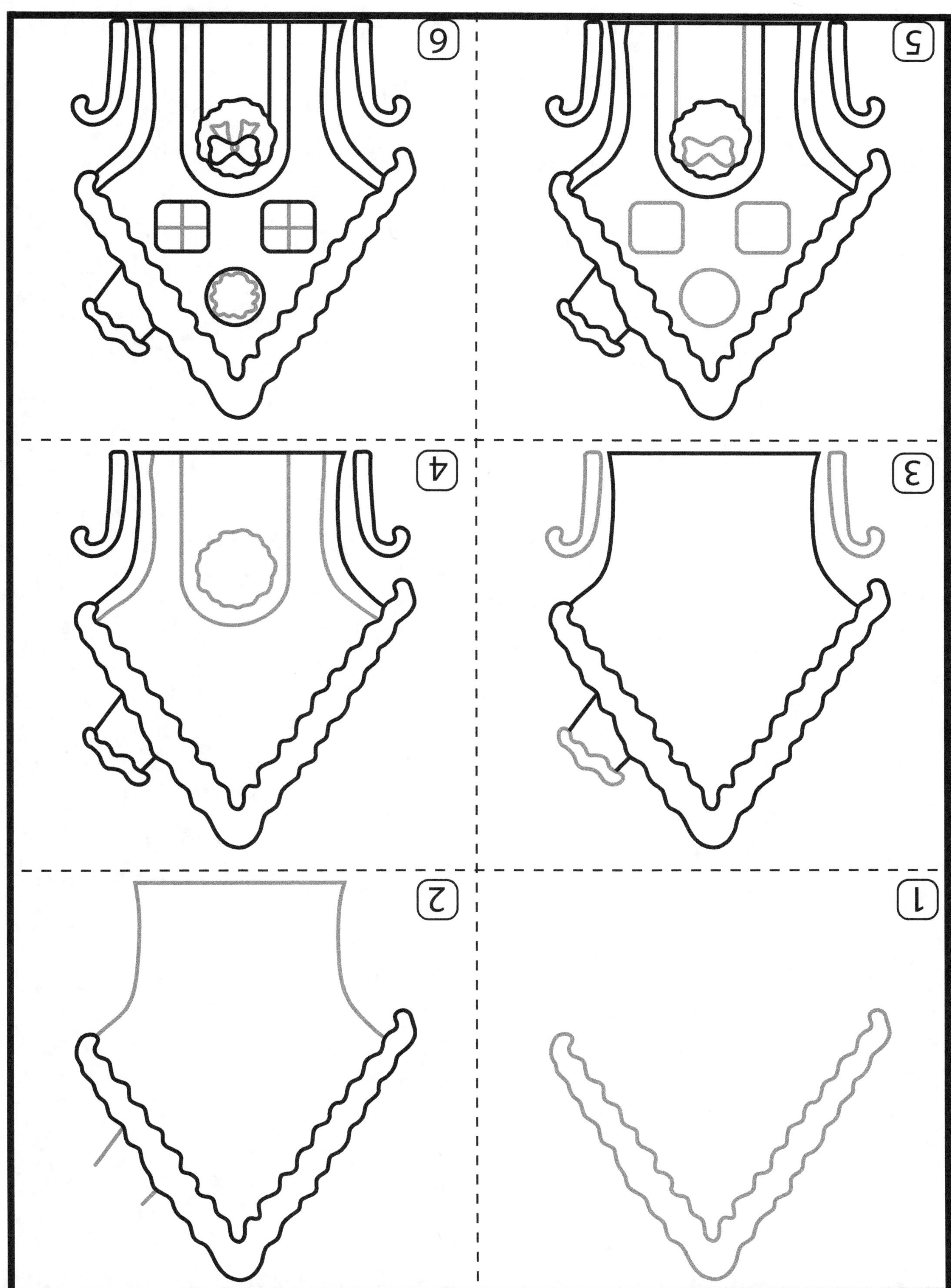

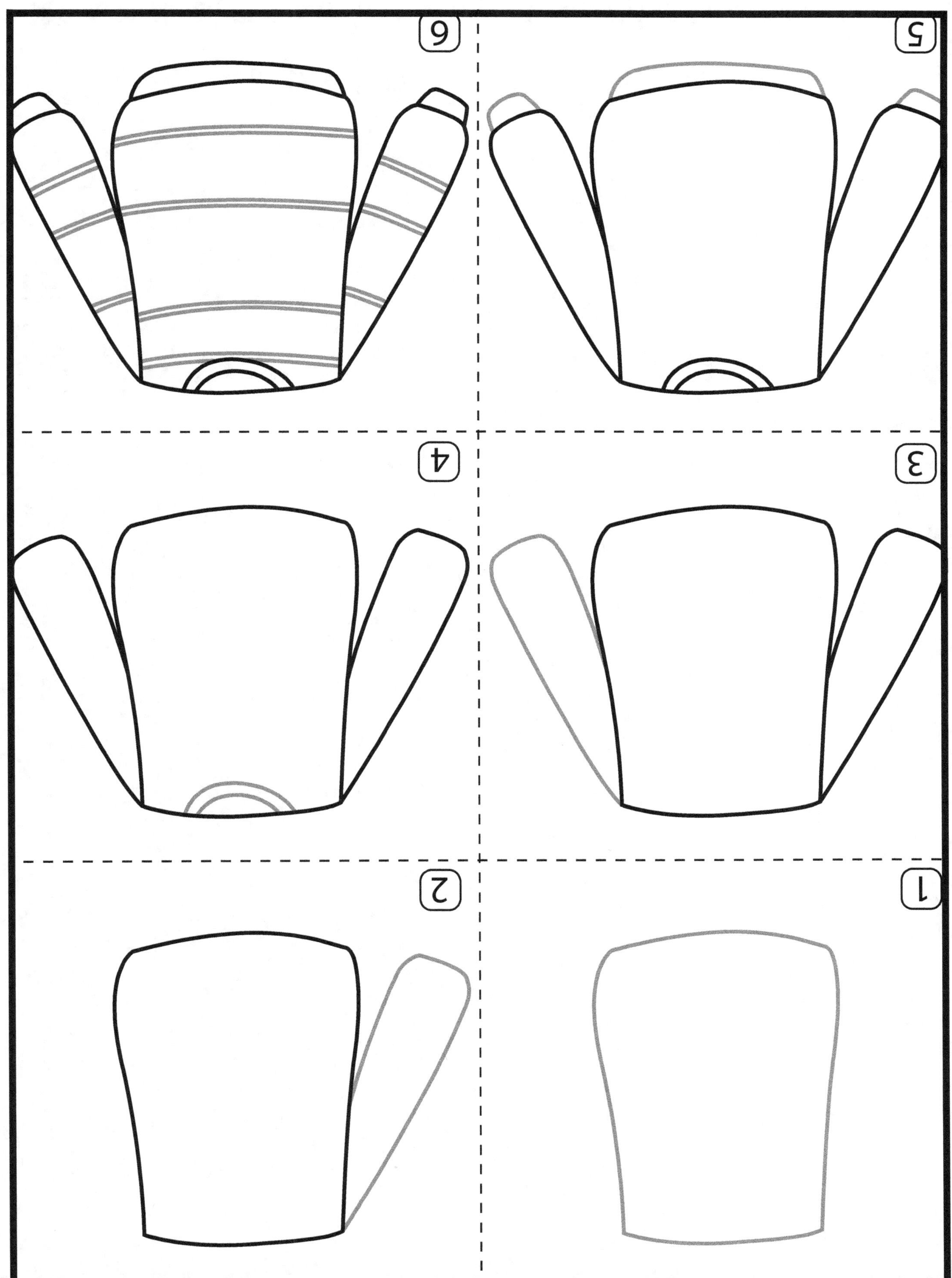

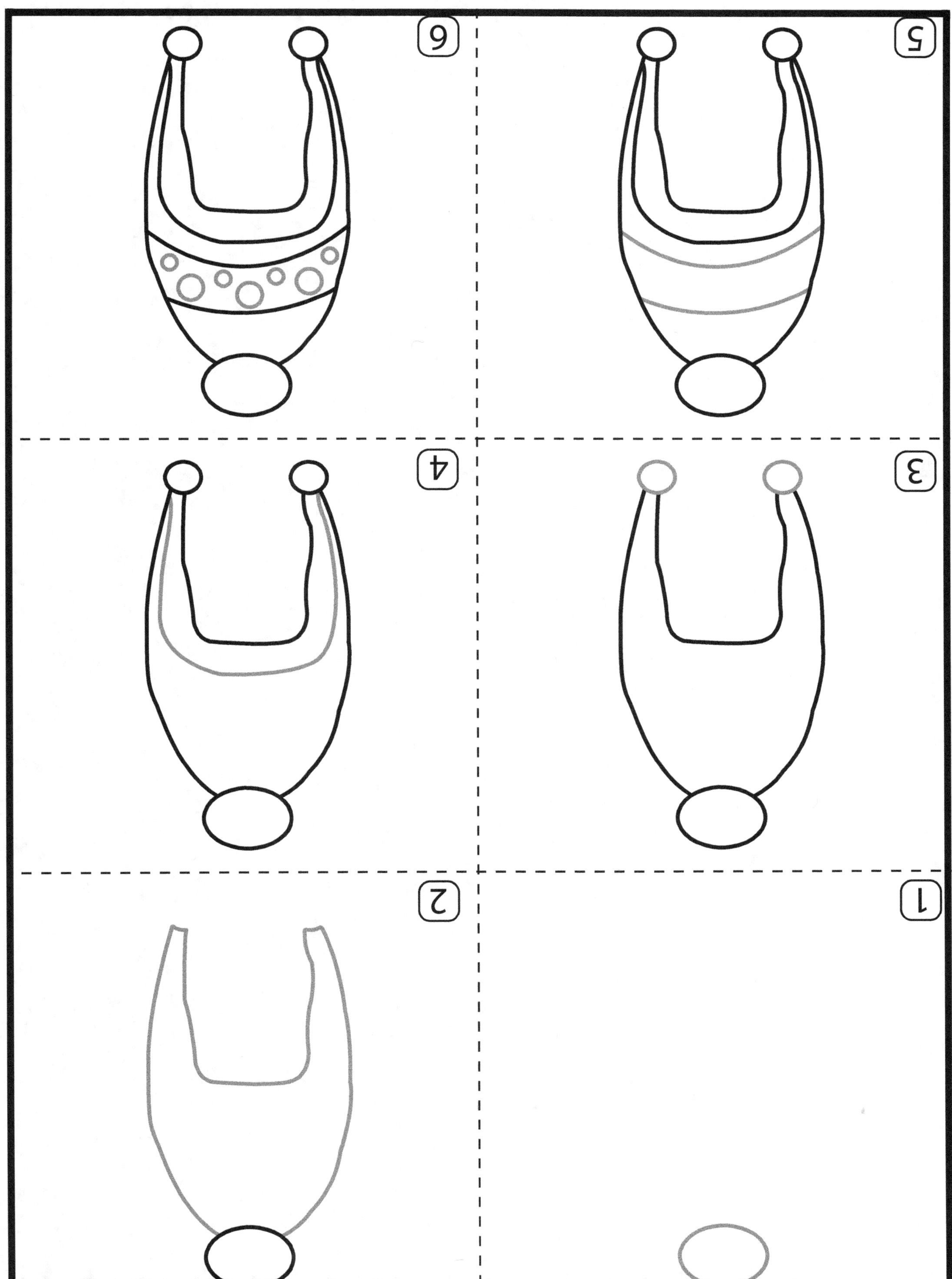

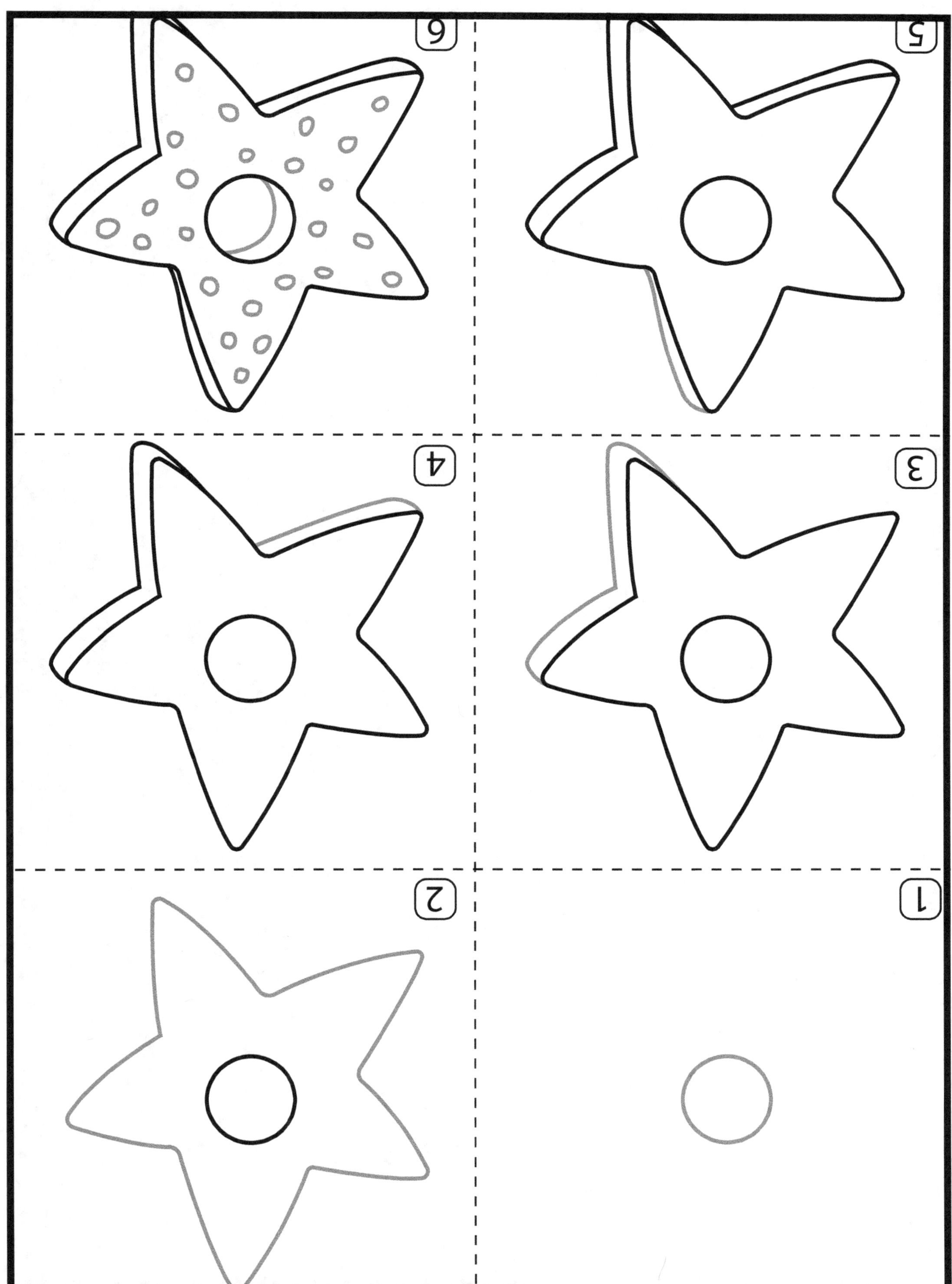

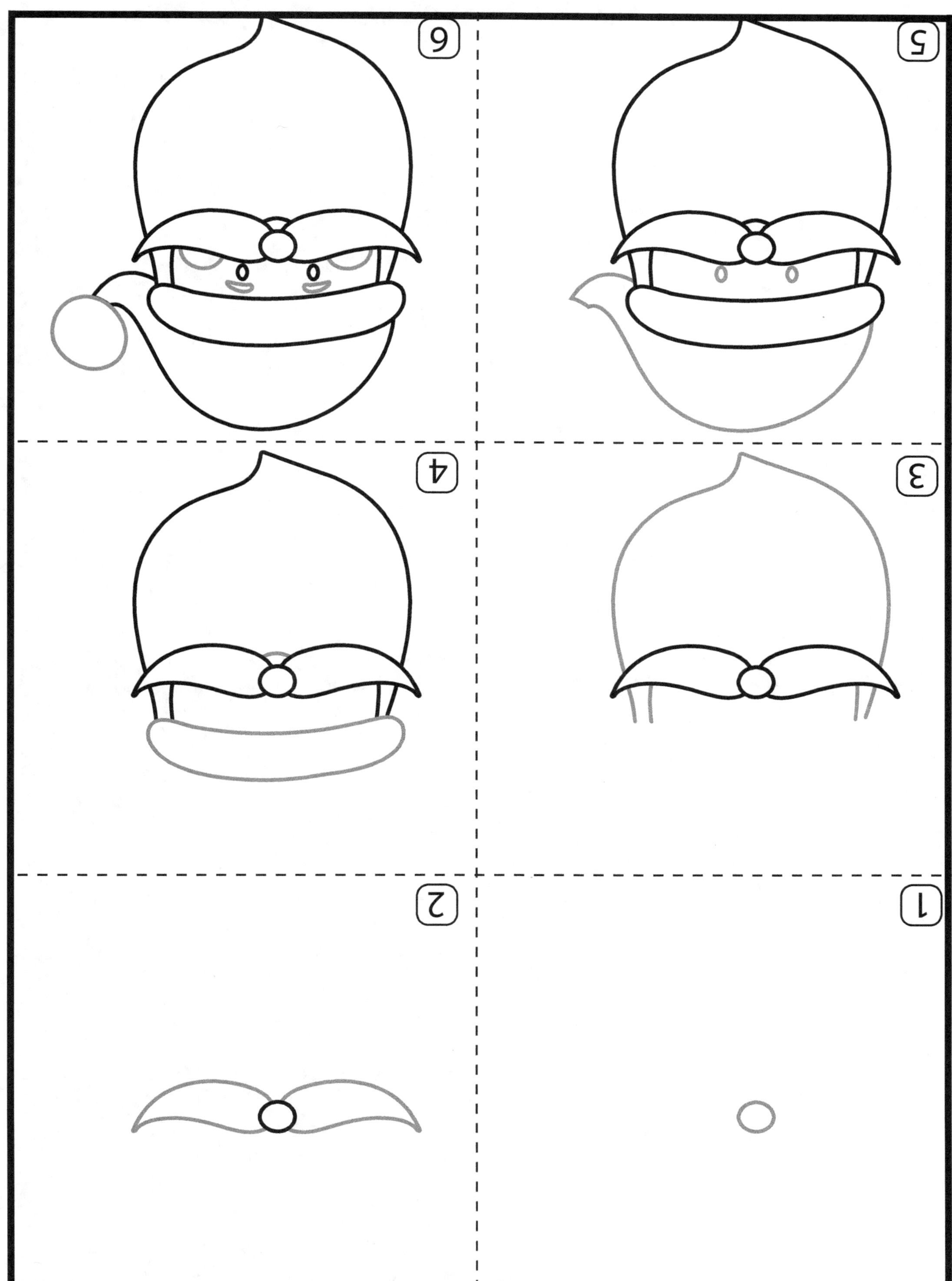

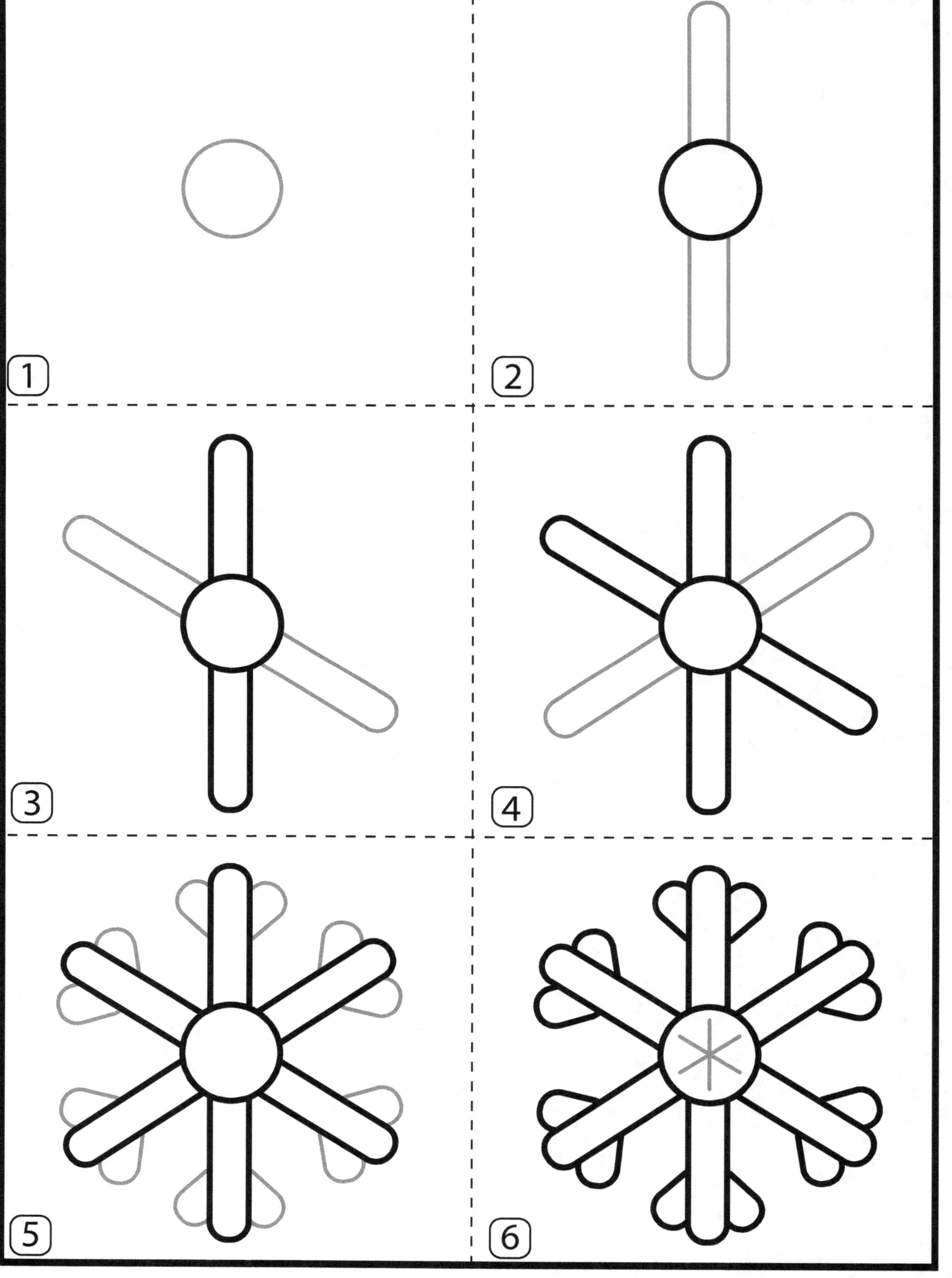

1
2
3
4
5
6

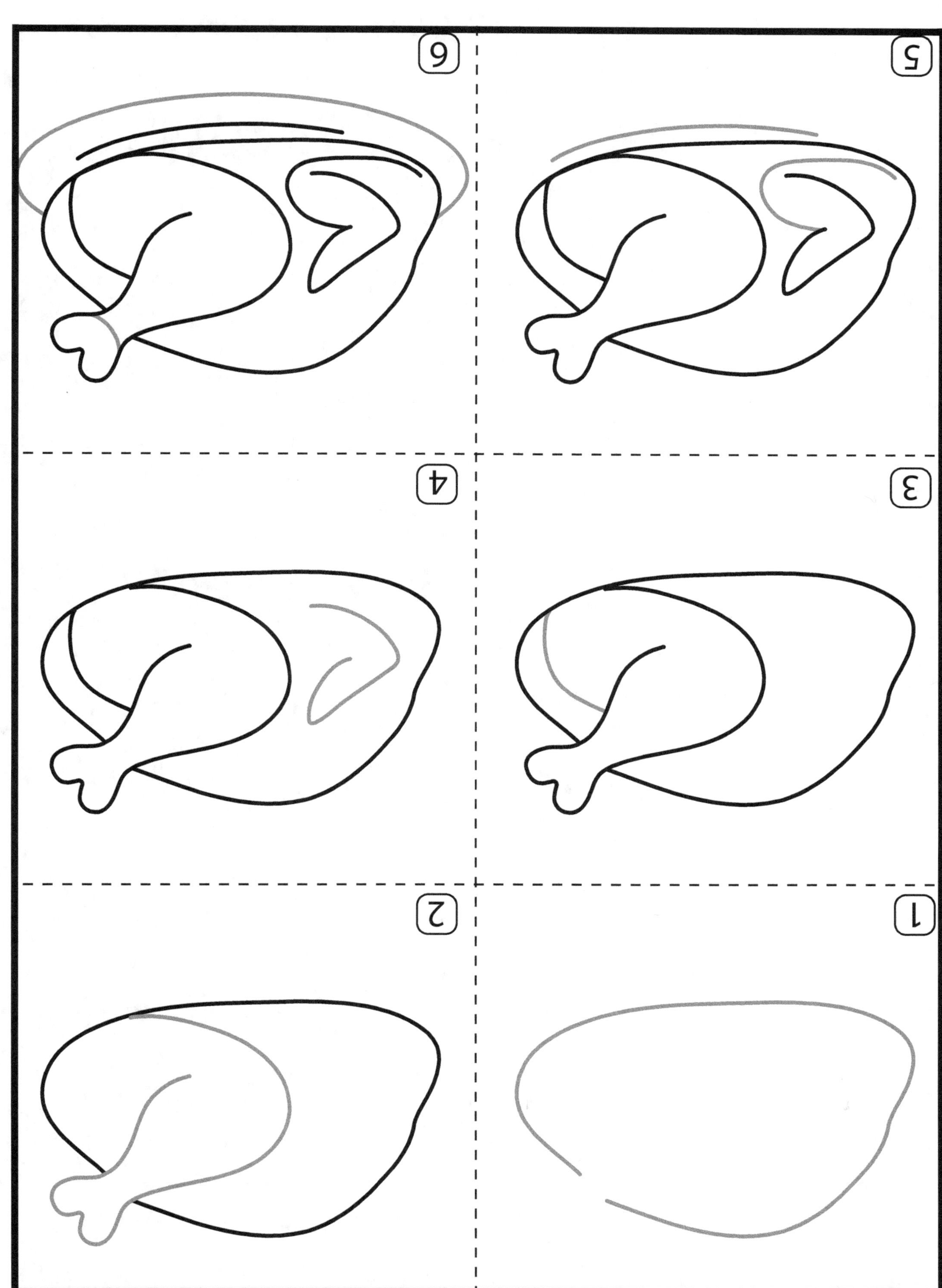

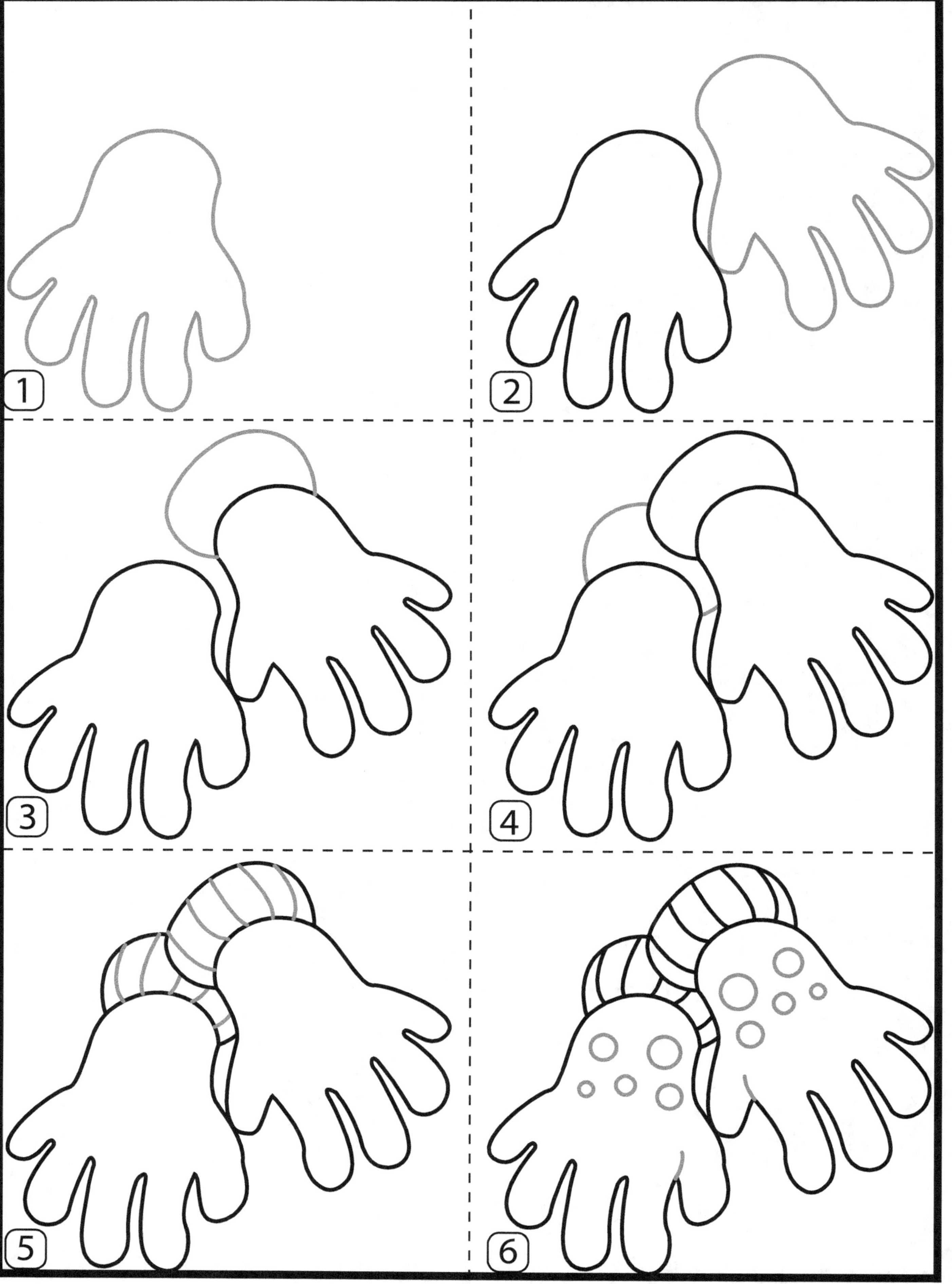

1
2
3
4
5
6